Introduction

Welcome to the United States of America

1 Find the places ▸ pp. 6–7

a) *Find and label the following places on the map. Use the map on the front inside cover of your student's book. You can also label other places you know.*

~~The Grand Canyon~~ • ~~Atlanta~~ • ~~New York~~ • ~~San Clemente~~ • ~~Hermann~~ • ~~Las Vegas~~

b) *In which US states are the following places? Find and complete the sentences.*

The Grand Canyon is in Arizona.
Atlanta is in Georgia.
Las Vegas is in Nevada.
San Clemente is in California.
Hermann is in Missouri.
Miami is in Florida.

Now you

Describe the picture on p. 7 of your student's book.
Use: **in the foreground**, **in the background**, **in the middle**, **at the bottom**, **in front of**, *etc.*

Ideas: **glass floor**, **canyon rim**, **awesome view**, **deep**, **wide**, **amazing**, **multi-coloured rock**, **see for miles**, **woman**, **look**, **arms**, *etc.*

Write a paragraph about 60 words in your exercise book.

Info box

The USA is the third largest country in the world. From the east to the west coast, it's about 4,300 km wide. The population[1] of the US is about 300 million.

[1] population [ˌpɒpju'leɪʃn] *Bevölkerung*

2 Four new faces ▸ p. 11

a) Write short profiles.

Name:	Madison	Jake	Catalin	Louis
Age:	14	14	14	14
Hometown:	Atlanta	Hermann	New York	San Clamate
State:	Georgia	Misouri	New Jersey	California

Test

b) What else do you know about the four students? Tick (✔) the correct box.

		Madison	Jake	Caitlin	Luis
1	Who made the trip to the Grand Canyon by car with his/her father?		✔		
2	Who flew to Las Vegas first?	✔			
3	Who went to the Grand Canyon with a youth group?				✔
4	Who travelled almost 2500 miles by car?			✔	
5	Who took Route 66 to the Grand Canyon?		✔		
6	Who rode with a mule train to the bottom of the Canyon?	✔			
7	Who camped at two different places on the rim?			✔	
8	Who did lots of jobs to get enough money for the trip?				✔
9	Who walked down into the canyon and saw a condor?		✔		
10	Who drove by car with the whole family for three and a half days to get to the Canyon?			✔	

3 WORDS The Grand Canyon puzzle ▸ p. 11

Complete with words from pp. 8–11.

1 The English word for 'eindrucksvoll, beeindruckend' is …

2 You can walk along the … of the Canyon.

3 If you … into the Canyon, wear strong shoes and take lots of water.

4 This American word describes the Grand Canyon.

5 Luis and his friends slept in a … and cooked their own food.

6 Rangers tell visitors about the … and human history of the park.

0303

1			G	r	A	n	d			
2					r	i	m			
3				h	i	k	e			
					z					
4	a				o					
5			T	e	n	t				
6					a					

4 The Grand Canyon: facts ▸ p. 11

Test

a) *Are the following statements right or wrong? Mark a number.*

	Statement	Right	Wrong
1	When you drive from New York to the Grand Canyon you cross four time zones.	70	75
2	Hualapai Indians still live in the Grand Canyon.	25	20
3	You are not allowed to camp in the Grand Canyon area.	54	35
4	The Grand Canyon is in the state of Nevada.	30	65
5	The river that goes through the Canyon is the Colorado River.	58	90
6	Las Vegas is in the same state as the Grand Canyon.	15	22
7	You can travel on 'Route 66' from Chicago to the Canyon.	36	43
8	You can take a mule train into the Canyon.	65	57
9	The job of the rangers is to protect the park and its visitors.	30	25
10	You are not allowed to hike into the Canyon.	65	35

b) *Add the ten numbers that are marked in a) and write the answer:* ________ *. The correct answer tells you how long the Grand Canyon is in kilometres. Check your answer in the* ***Info box*** *below.*

5 Luis's diary ▸ p. 11

Luis wrote a diary about his trip to the Grand Canyon. Read his school essay on p. 9 of your student's book again. What do you think Luis wrote in his diary? Write two sentences for each day. You can write about the bus journey, the hikes, the camping, the cooking, etc.

Info box

The Grand Canyon is:
- 446 km long
- between 6 and 24 km wide
- more than 1 km deep

Day 1: *The bus picked us up* ________________

Day 2: ________________

Day 3: ________________

Day 4: ________________

6 STUDY SKILLS Correcting mistakes ▸ p. 11 • SF (p. 155)

Find and mark the grammar and spelling mistakes. There's one in each sentence. Then write what is correct.

	Correct
1 Luis worked hardly to get enough money for his trip to the Grand Canyon.	hard
2 Jake and his dad have begun their journey on August 7.	have begin
3 Madison's parents didn't have much time for a vaccation this year.	vacation
4 On the bus journey Luis and his friends sang songs in spanish.	
5 Caitlins' hometown is New York.	Catlin's
6 The Park Rangers can give you lots of informations about the Canyon.	information
7 Tourists ask often questions about the natural and human history of the Canyon.	often
8 Caitlin writes dayly blogs from New York.	daylie
9 The multi-coloured walls of the Canyon look beautifully in the sun.	beautiful
10 Jake's dad is a good driver. He drives really good.	well
11 Route 66 is the famous road who goes from Chicago to L.A.	
12 Caitlin and her parents always go in summer to a national park.	

0506

Now you

Whose journey to the Grand Canyon do you think was the most interesting? Why? Write a few sentences.

I find the most interesting on the Grand Canyon is the beautiful candryside and the Colorado River there through of him flows.

7 Extra STUDY SKILLS WRITING Write a blog ▸ p. 11 • SF (pp. 154–155)

Imagine that you went to the Grand Canyon in your summer vacation. Use the information that Caitlin, Luis, Jake and Madison give about the Canyon and write your own blog (for ideas look at Caitlin's blog on p. 8 of your student's book). Write in your exercise book.

Remember:

- *brainstorm your ideas*
- *structure your text (beginning, middle, end)*
- *use paragraphs (a new paragraph for a new idea)*
- *structure your information (5 Ws)*
- *make your sentences interesting (linking words, adverbs)*
- *correct your text (grammar, spelling)*

0508

Unit 1 New York, New York

1 New York sights ► pp. 12–13

a) Write the names of the New York sights correctly and match them to the pictures.

2 tteuaS fo ieytbLr | 1 tfihF nAueve | 5 earCnlt karP
4 yorklBon gderiB | 6 iaonnwthC | 3 pmreEi tteaS iilgunBd

1 Fifth Avenue

2 the Statue of Liberty

3 the Empire State Building

0601

4 the Brooklyn Bridge

5 Central Park

6 China town

b) What other places have you heard of in New York City? Write a list.

I have also heard of Central park, Statue of Liberty, Empire State Building, Brooklin Bridge.

2 Blue box: New York's five boroughs ► p. 13, p. 175

a) What do you know about New York's boroughs? Right or Wrong? Mark a letter.

		Right	Wrong
1	Brooklyn is the biggest New York borough.	S	E
2	New York's highest buildings are in Manhattan.	L	T
3	Brooklyn Bridge links Brooklyn to Staten Island.	A	L
4	Queens is in the south-west of Long Island.	I	T
5	The Bronx is south of Manhattan.	E	S
6	There's a ferry between Staten Island and Manhattan.	I	M
7	Manhattan's streets usually have numbers, not names.	S	L
8	Central Park is in Queens.	H	L
9	Brooklyn and Queens are on Long Island.	A	T
10	New York Harbor is east of Manhattan.	S	N
11	Manhattan is an island between the Hudson and the East River.	D	N

b) If your answers are correct, you have written the name of another famous New York island:

ELLISISLAND

3 Blue box: British English – American English (1)

▸ p. 14, p. 175

a) *Which is British English? Which is American English? Find and write pairs.*

mobile phone	pavement	subway	line
queue	holiday(s)	petrol	downtown
underground	city centre	(school) year	sidewalk
cellphone	lift	elevator	chips
French fries	grade	vacation	gas

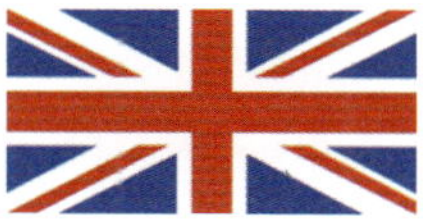

British English		American English	British English		American English
mobile phone	–	*cellphone*	pavement	–	sidewalk
queue	–	line	petrol	–	Gas
underground		subway	year	–	grade
holiday	–	vacation	lift	–	elevator
city Centre	–	downtown	French fries	–	chips

0703

b) *Underline the word in each sentence that is different in American English. Then write the word with AE spelling.*

I write travelled

I write traveled

1 Last year I travelled to New York – by plane, of course.	*traveled*
2 Travelling is exciting!	Traveling
3 Of course I went to a theatre on Broadway.	theater
4 I saw my favourite musical, *The Phantom of the Opera*.	
5 Did you know that Broadway is about 29 kilometres long?	Kilometers
6 Of course we did a harbour trip too.	harbor
7 Just imagine! The Statue of Liberty is 93 metres high!	

4 LISTENING[1] All about … getting around an American city

▸ p. 14 • SF (p. 148) Track 2

Test

You want to go to the Brooklyn Bridge. Listen. Which person gives you the right directions? A, B or C?

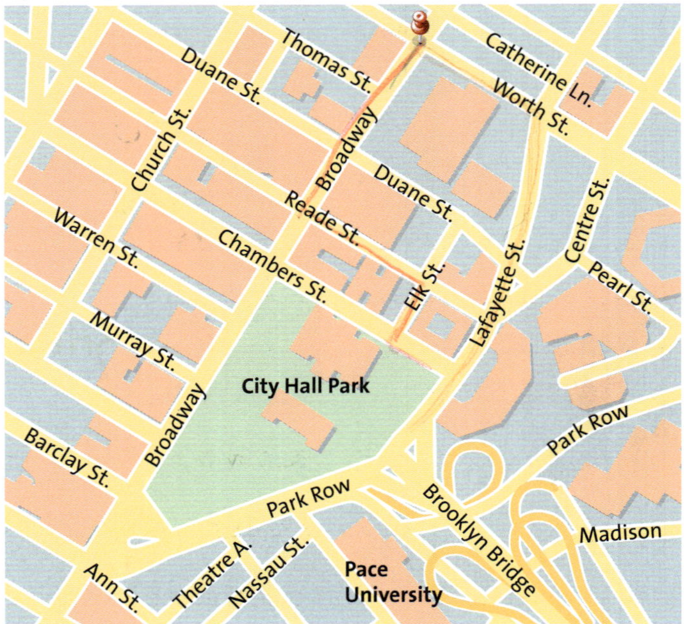

The person who gives the right directions is ___ .

5 LISTENING Blue box: American English (II)

▸ p. 14, p. 178 • SF (p. 148) Track 3

a) Different words

*Listen to the words. Are the words you hear British or American English? Write **BE** or **AE** after the number.*

1 ______ 4 ______

2 ______ 5 ______

3 ______ 6 ______

b) Different pronunciation

*Listen to the words. Is the pronunciation you hear British or American English? Write **BE** or **AE** after the number.*

1 ______ 4 ______

2 ______ 5 ______

3 ______ 6 ______

6 WORDS Verbs and nouns that go together

▸ p. 14

Tourists in New York do these things:

***a)** Match the verbs to the nouns.*

ask	souvenirs, tickets, a map
buy	a museum, the sights
write	a taxi, the subway, a bus tour
take	postcards
visit	the way, the time

***b)** Complete the sentences with words from a).*

1 If you ______ the subway, you won't see much.

2 To find the way more easily, you could buy ______ .

3 If you get lost[2], ask ______ .

4 Don't forget to ______ the Guggenheim Museum!

5 Tourists always write ______ to their families and friends.

[1] opposite ['ɒpəzɪt] *gegenüber* [2] get lost *sich verlaufen*

7 Sightseeing (Gerund as subject) ▸ p. 15 • GF 1a–b (p. 161)

a) Write the -ing-form (gerund) of the verbs. Be careful with the spelling!

plan –	planning	shop –	shopping
get –	getting	visit –	visiting
cycle –	cycling	walk –	walking
run –	running	write –	writeing

b) Complete what Ryan and Caitlin say with the correct gerunds from a).

Ryan Planning things to do in New York is fun. I'm really excited. How are we going to get around?

Caitlin Well, ________ around the city is best by bus or subway. ________ everywhere makes your feet tired and ________ in city traffic isn't healthy.

Info box

New York City is often called 'The Big Apple' or 'The city that never sleeps'. Eight million people live there, and it's the biggest city in the USA. On the streets of New York about 170 languages are spoken.

Ryan But ________ in Central Park is healthy. Can we do that too?

Caitlin Sure, but isn't ________ all the famous sights more important?

Ryan Well, we can do all that first. And ________ at Macy's[1] is important too. I need some presents and postcards for my friends.

0907 *Caitlin* ________ postcards is boring. But I'm sure we'll have enough time for Macy's!

8 WORDS Job talk ▸ p. 15

a) Choose from the box and write the correct job names under the pictures.

actor • caretaker • coach • ranger • singer • engineer • editor • artist • film-maker • firefighter • waiter • paramedic • TV presenter

1 
____

2 

actor

3 
____

4 
____

5 
____

6 

____

7 

____

8 
____

0908

b) **Extra** *Which is the most interesting job? Why do you think so? Which of the jobs is the most boring? Why do you think so? In your exercise book, write two texts of about 50 words each.*

I think the ... has the most interesting job because ... I think the ... has the most boring job because ...

[1] Macy's ['meɪsiːz] *großes Kaufhaus in New York*

9 He loves being a firefighter (Gerund as object)

▸ p. 15 • GF 2b (p. 161)

a) *The gerund (-ing-form) is used after certain verbs. Underline the verb that comes before the gerund. Then use a gerund of the verb in brackets.*

1 Caitlin's dad loves *being* (be) a New York firefighter.

2 He doesn't like geting up (get up) in the middle of the night.

3 But he can't imagine doing (do) anything else.

4 He enjoys spending (spend) time with the men and women at the fire station.

5 Caitlin loves rideing (ride) her bike round Central Park in the rain.

b) *Choose a verb from the box and use it as a gerund.*

chat • look • take • sit • shop + ing

1 Caitlin's mom really likes shopping at Macy's.

2 Caitlin enjoys taking visitors up the Empire State Building.

3 Ryan hated siting in a plane for six hours.

4 He didn't like looking at clouds for hours.

1009 5 But he enjoyed ~~looking~~ chating to the girl next to him.

10 WRITING My trip to the ESB

▸ p. 16 • SF (pp. 154–155)

Imagine you went up the Empire State Building. In your exercise book, write a short report about your visit (80–100 words). Read p. 16 of your student's book again for ideas.

Remember the steps of writing:

1 Brainstorming ideas
- collect ideas and put them in order (in a list, mind map)
- answer the questions Who? What? When? Where? Why? and maybe How? (in a chart)

2 Writing
- structure your text (beginning, middle, end)
- use paragraphs and topic sentences
- write better sentences with adjectives, adverbs, time phrases, linking words

3 Correcting your text
- think carefully about spelling (take > taking, plan > planned, half > halves)
- about grammar (tenses, verb endings, irregular verbs, word order)

These phrases will help you:

In the summer holidays • New York • I visited my e-friend • very excited • The weather was great so ... • At the ticket office we ... • My friend told me some ESB facts • we went up in a fast lift • lots of visitors • funny feeling in my stomach • When we got to the top, I ... • took lots of photos • After that we ... • Later ... • bought postcards and souvenirs • We started to feel hungry, so ... • had a snack in the café • a fun day • the ESB is the most exciting building I have ever seen

11 READING COURSE

Part 1: Visit downtown New York (Working out the meaning of words)

▸ p. 16 • SF (p. 150)

a) Read this part of a tourist brochure. Think about the underlined words.

Visit downtown New York

Some things have changed, but a lot have remained the same in downtown New York. It's an important center of commerce and has more than 300 years of history.

Downtown has everything: art and museums, architecture, skyscrapers, concert halls, great shopping, lots of restaurants, entertainment and fantastic waterfront. Don't miss the sunset over the Hudson.

There are so many sights to see. The excitement and energy of the city are never-ending.

You can reach downtown by bus, car or subway. It takes only 20 minutes to walk from the Hudson to the East River. Why not take a luxury ride in a stretch limo?

The food downtown is varied, as people who have settled here will tell you. It is served leisurely or fast. You can eat indoors or out. Or why not dine in elegance? Get a hot dog from a street vendor or a snack from a supermarket. And you'll never be bored. There's always lots of fun with exciting events. Just enjoy the sounds and smells of downtown New York.

b) What helps you to understand the new words? Read 1–4 below and write the words in four lists:

1 The pictures help me to understand these words:

vendor (Straßenverkäufer), stretch limo,

2 These words look like German words:

commerce (Kommerz/Handel), architecture (Architektur), luxury (luxuriös), elegance (eleganz)

3 I can understand these words from the context:

changed (verändert),

4 I already know a part of the word or a word from the word family:

waterfront (Hafengebiet),

12 Liam (Gerunds after prepositions) ► p. 16 • GF 1c (p. 162)

a) *Ryan's cousin Liam in Ireland talks about his time in New York. Underline the word and the preposition that comes before the gerund and choose an -ing-form from the box to complete the sentence.*

living • *going* • getting • moving

'I had the chance[1] of *going* to New York on a student exchange. It was great, and now I'm even interested in moving a job there. I'm a bit fed up with living in our village, and I have often thought of getting to another country.'

b) *Use a gerund of the verbs in brackets.*

'I really like the idea of working (work) in a big city like New York. At first I might be a bit scared of being (be) alone, but I could visit my exchange family. I'm quite good at making (make) friends and I'd have the chance of meeting (meet) lots of new people.

c) *Choose a verb from the box and use it as a gerund.*

dance • fall • join • live • ride • visit

'I would find out about visiting a sports club or a youth group. I like discos and I'm not bad at dancing. When I was a kid, I was quite good at riding too, but I haven't ridden for years, so I'd be scared of falling off the horse! I'm really interested in joining all New York's

1212 museums and art galleries too. I'd never be tired of living in the city that never sleeps.'

13 About you (Mixed gerunds) ► p. 16 • GF 1 (pp. 161–162)

Complete the sentences with gerunds. Use the ideas in the green box or your own ideas.

1 *Having fun with friends* makes me happy.

2 ______ makes me nervous.

3 In my free time I love hanging out with friends.

4 At the weekends I really enjoy ______

5 I can't imagine ______

6 Sometimes I'm scared of doing badly in a test.

7 I'm really interested in ______

8 I'm good at reading books.

1213 9 I'm really fed up with ______

- *have fun with friends*
- help in the kitchen
- visit museums
- watch horror films
- ~~hang out with friends~~
- ~~read books~~
- live in another country
- be alone at home
- get e-mails from friends
- ~~do badly in a test~~
- do English exercises
- get presents
- eat spicy food
- tell jokes
- speak English
- live in a small village/ big city

[1] chance [tʃɑːns] *Chance, Möglichkeit*

14 REVISION Ruthie's e-mail (if and when) ▸ p. 17

*Ruthie writes this e-mail to a friend in the UK. Complete it with **if** or **when**.*

Hi Cathy!
Have to tell you my exciting news! Ryan (my friend's cousin from Ireland) has arrived – and he's just great!
My cousin from Texas is coming soon. I've already made a plan of places to go *when* she's here.
You said you would like to visit New York, so just come! If you came, you could share my room – it's quite big. If you came in summer, there would be lots to do. If you came in winter, we could go Christmas shopping together. When I go shopping with friends, we usually go to Macy's. You have to see it when you're here. Mom always says when you wanted a white elephant, Macy's would get it for you! Oh, and when Ryan asks me out, I'll say YES!
Write soon, Ruthie

1314

15 EVERYDAY ENGLISH MEDIATION Asking the way ▸ p. 17 • SF (p. 152)

Test

You are in New York. A young German tourist asks you the way to Times Square, but you don't know, so you ask an American woman on the street. Help the tourist.

Info box

Times Square

Times Square got its name from the New York Times newspaper building, which stood there in 1904.
Today you find bright lights, cinemas, theatres, shops, bars and restaurants there.

You Excuse me, this guy is a tourist and he wants to go to Times Square. I'm a tourist too. So can you help him?

Woman Times Square? That's easy. It's at Broadway and 43rd. He could take the subway. But the bus would be quicker. It's just a few stops.

You Sie sagt, ____________

Tourist Nein, ich kenne mich nicht aus. Ich gehe lieber zu Fuß. Frag sie bitte, wie weit es ist.

You He says ____________

Woman OK. You go straight down Broadway, that way. I guess it's 8 or 9 blocks, maybe even 10.

You ____________

Tourist OK. Und wie lange werde ich zu Fuß brauchen? Ich treffe jemanden in einer halben Stunde.

You ____________

Woman Yes, that's long enough. He should do it easily. And there's lots to see on the way.

You ____________

1315

Tourist Thank you und tschüss!

16 EVERYDAY ENGLISH SPEAKING Visiting Liberty ▸ p. 17 Track 4

Test

It's your first day in New York. Your exchange partner Todd asks you what you would like to do first. You'd like to see the Statue of Liberty.
Listen to Todd and give suitable[1] answers or comments in the pauses. Say as much as you can. Use the ideas below or your own ideas. For more information read the ***Fun fact*** *box on this page. Do the exercise at least twice.*

1 you want to see everything – start with Liberty

2 yes, of course – from parents – last birthday

3 read a lot – know some details (see Fun fact!)

4 yes – school history lessons – immigration station

Fun fact

The Statue of Liberty …
- was born on 28th October 1886.
- is 93 m tall.
- weighs[2] 204,100 kilos.

Her nose is almost 1.5 m long.
Her feet are 7.6 m long, so she takes size 879 sandals[3]!
You can climb 354 stairs (22 floors) to the crown[4], but since 9/11 it has been closed to visitors.

Just for fun

Why does the Statue of Liberty stand in New York Harbor? – Because she can't sit down.

17 WORDS New York puzzle ▸ p. 17

Write the answers in the puzzle and find a famous name for New York.

1 This New York borough has a famous zoo. The …

2 New Yorkers often buy food and coffee to go here.

3 The name for the place where the towers of the World Trade Center stood is '… Zero'.

4 New Yorkers often have this for breakfast.

5 This is the name for Manhattan's tall buildings.

6 The 'E' in ESB means …

7 A famous bridge links this borough to Manhattan.

1417 8 The bridge in 7 goes over the … River.

1	Bronx
2	cafe
3	Ground
4	Bagle
5	Skyscrapers
6	Empire
7	Brooklyn
8	East

Extra Now you

What do you know about 'Ground Zero'? Make notes to prepare a short talk[5] for your English class. Use the information on p. 15 of your student's book and look for more information on the internet. Practise your talk at home. Your friend/parents/sister/brother could listen to you.

[1] suitable ['sju:təbl] *passend* [2] weigh [weɪ] *wiegen*
[3] sandal ['sændl] *Sandale* [4] crown [kraʊn] *Krone*
[5] talk *Rede*

18 EXTRA Background File A COUNTRY OF IMMIGRANTS ▸ pp. 18–19

a) *What do you know about Ellis Island and US immigrants? Read p. 18 in your student's book again and tick (✔) the correct answer, A, B or C. Sometimes more than one answer is correct. You need the letters in brackets in b).*

1 When was the Ellis Island Immigration Station opened?

A 1892. (S) B 1900. (I) C 1921. (H)

2 Why did immigrants want to go to America?

A They were very poor at home. (I)
B For reasons of religion or politics. (S)
C The US paid immigrant workers well. (T)

3 How many immigrants came to the US between 1892 and 1924?

A 4 million. (L) B More than 12 million. (A) C 12,000. (A)

4 What is Ellis Island today?

A An immigration station. (G) B A castle. (L) C A museum. (U)

5 When was Ellis Island finally closed?

A 1924. (Y) B 1890. (S) C 1954. (R)

b) *The letters after the correct answers in a) tell you the name of a country where many immigrants came from. Put the letters in the correct order.*

The country is ______________________.

c) *Read the statements of the young immigrants on p. 19 of your student's book, then match the names to the statements 1–4. Who said what?*

1 This person felt very small when he/she first saw the building on Ellis Island. It was much bigger than the houses in the town he/she had come from. It was C ______________________.

2 This immigrant said that the only thing people spoke about was a new life in America.

It was ______________________.

3 This person said they were all strangers in the USA, so nobody felt like a stranger.

It was ______________________.

4 This immigrant said the terrible storms at sea had made everybody very sick.

It was ______________________.

d) *Use the information on pp. 18–19 of your student's book and write 80–100 words on the topic 'Immigration to the USA in the past and today'. You can use the website www.ellisisland.org to find out more information.*
Write in your exercise book. Remember:

- *brainstorming*
- *the 5 Ws*
- *beginning, middle, end*
- *correcting your text*

19 WORKING WITH THE TEXT You can tell me ▸ pp. 26–28

a) *Read the text on pp. 26–28 of your student's book again. Then describe these pictures in two or three sentences each. Say what is happening and why.*

1

2

1 In picture 1 Kelly and Anthony are coming out of the subway.

2 In picture 2 Kelly and Anthony are sitting

b) *How did they feel? Find a part in the story where …*

1 Anthony felt nervous: I think Anthony felt nervous when the two guys came up to him and Kelly in the park. The guys looked dangerous. (ll. 76–90)

2 Anthony felt angry:

3 Anthony felt sad:

4 Kelly felt sad:

c) *Use these words to make true sentences about the events[1]. Write a sentence each.*

1 feel sick: Anthony felt sick because of the noise and the smells in the subway.

2 tears:

3 blood:

4 cab:

5 bench:

d) **Extra** *What do you learn about the two teenagers in the story? Write a short description of Kelly or Anthony in your exercise book (about 80 words). First collect information from the text and find adjectives (scared, friendly, brave) that you can use in your description. Remember to structure your text (use paragraphs, beginning, middle, end).*

[1] event [ɪ'vent] *Ereignis*

1 American English. What are these places?

1 You can buy sandwiches, snacks or coffee to go here. ______

2 This is what Americans call the city centre. ______

3 You can see lots of these very tall buildings in American cities. ______

4 This is what Americans call a group of buildings between two streets. ______

5 Americans usually live here if they don't live in a house. ______

1701 6 In the US you buy petrol here. ______

2 British and American English. Write the missing words.

BE		AE	BE		AE
1 ground floor	–	first floor	4 rucksack	–	backpack
2 timetable	–	schedule	5 rubbish	–	garbage
3 (school) year	–	grade	6 chips	–	French fries

1702

3 **If** or **when**? Put in the correct word.

1 I'm flying to New York tomorrow. I'll call you ______ I get to the hotel.

2 ______ the weather's good, I'll see all the sights on foot.

1703 3 I'm going to visit Ellis Island. I'll collect lots of information ______ I'm there.

4 Complete the sentences with gerunds.

1 Caitlin really liked ______ (plan) a sightseeing tour of New York for Ryan.

2 Caitlin had the idea of ______ (meet) Ruth for lunch at Ruth's local deli.

3 Ryan was very interested in ______ (find) out about his uncle's life as a New York firefighter.

4 Ryan enjoyed ______ (take) photos from the top of the Empire State Building.

1704 5 When Ryan was back in Ireland, he often talked about ______ (travel) to New York again.

20 points

Now you

1705 1706 *Prepare a three-minute talk about the good and bad things about life in a big city like New York. Make notes or a mind map first. You can use the information in Unit 1 of your student's book and/or information from the internet.*

Here are some exercises that will help you with your practice test 1.

1 WORDS City travel ▸ *pp. 30–31*

a) *In your exercise book, make a 'city travel' network. Look at the pictures for ideas. Use different types of words (nouns, adjectives, verbs).*

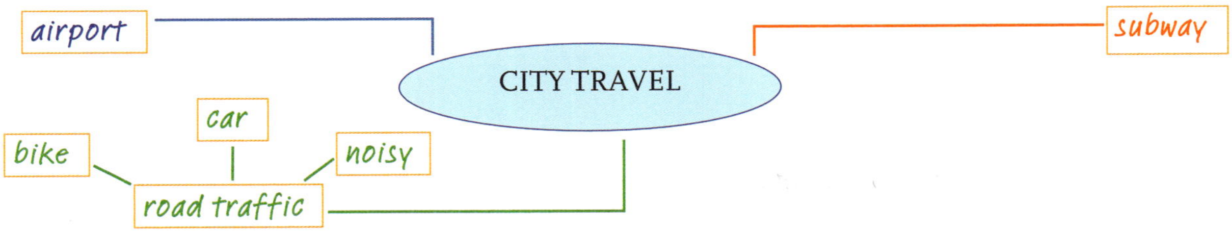

b) *Choose picture A, B or C and describe it in a paragraph. Use:* ***in the foreground/background, on the right****, etc.*

Picture A shows a scene at an airport. ______________________________

____

____

____

____

____

____

2 The city that never sleeps (Simple present or present progressive) ▸ *pp. 30–31*

Complete with the correct verb form: simple present or present progressive

1 The first thing that tourists *visit* (visit) in New York is the Statue of Liberty or the ESB.

2 Most tourists ______________ (not have) enough time for the museums or the parks.

3 I often ______________ (eat) at a deli. I usually ______________ (have) a bagel with cream cheese. Delicious!

4 I ______________ (go) to my favourite deli right now. My friends ______________ (wait) for me there.

5 It ______________ (rain) now, but later we ______________ (go) to Central Park to hang out.

6 Life in New York ______________ (not get) boring because it's the city that never ______________ (sleep).

3 A trip to Macy's (Simple past or past progressive) ▸ pp. 30–31

Underline the correct verb form.

Anna, a British exchange student, (stayed/was staying) in New York. Kelly, Anna's exchange partner, (wanted/was wanting) to show her Macy's. Just as they (were crossing/crossed) W 34th Street, Kelly (was saying/said): 'I have to go somewhere for Mom first. I'll meet you in Macy's on the first floor near the elevators in fifteen minutes. OK?' First, Anna (looked/was looking) at some trendy bags and some funny postcards. Then she (went/was going) to the meeting place. She (was waiting/waited) – 10 minutes, 15 minutes, 20 minutes. But Kelly (didn't arrive/wasn't arriving). What was wrong? Anna (was deciding/decided) to look for Kelly outside. Just as Anna (was walking/walked) down the stairs to the main door, she suddenly (saw/was seeing) Kelly. She (stood/was standing) near the elevators. 'But Kelly! You said the first floor! That's one floor up.' 'No, Anna. **This** is the first floor. You were on the second floor!'

4 STUDY SKILLS Correcting mistakes ▸ pp. 30–31 • SF (p. 155)

This is Jürgen's e-mail to a friend in the States. Mark and correct his mistakes.

Hi Todd!
Last week we have come to Berlin. We visit my grandparents here. On Monday we have seen the Reichstag. It was great. Maybe tomorrow we go to the zoo because I enjoy to watch wild animals. We also saw the Brandenburg Gate and I made a lot of photos.
My dad is born in Berlin. When he was a child, lived he in the east part of the city. He has told us a lot over the history from the city.
Just now we sit in a café on the Ku'damm. Dad is takeing photos and my sister is shoping. You should visit Berlin too. You'd like it here...

Correct
came,

5 When I'm in a big city, ... (Gerunds) ▸ pp. 30–31 • GF 1 (pp. 161–162)

Complete the sentences. Use a gerund and ideas from the box or your own ideas.

When I'm in a big city for the first time, ...

1 I always enjoy *exploring.* ____________________

2 I'm always interested in ____________________

3 I'm sometimes a bit scared of ____________________

4 I love ____________________

5 I hate ____________________

6 I'm always excited about ____________________

- *explore*
- get lost
- look round ...
- see the sights
- visit museums
- take a bus tour
- see new places
- wait in queues

Unit 2 California, the 'Golden State'?

1 About California ▸ pp. 34–35

Test

a) Which statements are right? Which are wrong? Mark a letter.

	Statement	Right	Wrong
1	California is on the east coast of the USA.	M	S
2	Highway 101 takes you along the Californian coast.	A	O
3	California has five national parks.	N	C
4	The state north of California is Oregon.	R	T
5	The Golden Gate Bridge is in Los Angeles.	E	A
6	California is earthquake country.	M	R
7	Mexicans cross the US border to find work.	E	Y
8	Los Angeles and Las Vegas are both in California.	S	N
9	Hollywood is part of San Francisco.	Y	T
10	California produces lots of fruit and vegetables.	O	E

2001

b) If your answers are correct, you have written the name of California's state capital:

S ____________________

2 WORDS Synonyms ▸ p. 35

a) Match the synonyms.

until	apartment
mate	woods
flat	till
forest	middle
centre	friend

talk about	awful
terrible	start
equipment	be quiet
begin	discuss
shut up	gear

b) Where can you use a synonym in the following sentences? Mark the word in each sentence that you can change. Then write the synonym.

1 We talked about the problems of immigrants in school today. → discussed

2 California is a great place for sports, so you need lots of sports equipment. → ____________

3 What time does school start in the US? → ____________

2002

4 We talk too much in our English class. The teacher often tells us to shut up. → ____________

3 READING COURSE Part 2: Hollywood Studios (Skimming and scanning) ▸ p. 35 • SF (p. 150)

a) Match the information to the two reading skills.

Skimming

Scanning

- It helps you to find specific information.
- You move your eyes over the page – down and up or in an 'S'.
- You look at the title and words in bold print, pictures and captions.
- You think of the key words you are looking for and try and picture them.
- You can read the first and last sentence of each paragraph quickly.
- It helps you to find the main ideas of a text quickly.
- You don't read the whole text.

b) You are in L.A. with your family and you want to go to Hollywood Studios theme park. You would like to take ***some rides****,* ***learn about special effects****, maybe* ***see a movie star****. Can you do all that?* ***Skim*** *the page of the theme park's brochure below and find out.*

c) You need some specific information so you have to ***scan*** *the brochure to find it. Which key words will you look for? First mark them in the following questions, then scan the brochure. Write* ***Y*** *(Yes) or* ***N*** *(No).*

1 Can you take a tour of the studios? Y

2 Can you go behind the scenes? ____

3 Can you find out how they do special effects? ____

4 Can you have lunch with a star? ____

5 Can you buy tickets online? ____

6 Is the theme park open on Sundays? ____

Come to Hollywood Studios Theme Park, your ticket to the world of movies!

Take a studio tour!
Our studio tour is world famous! Meet life-like characters[1] close up. Come face to face with living dinosaurs! Meet King Kong! Get ready for a fantastic Hollywood movie experience[2] you'll never forget!

See the action!
Go behind the scenes of your favorite movies and TV shows. See real Hollywood movie-making, film sets[3] of the world's greatest movies!

Say 'Hi' to a star!
See a working studio where Hollywood movies are made. Take an inside look at what's filming! Big movie stars work here daily so you may get lucky and see your favorite star right in front of you. Don't forget to say 'Hi'!

Special effects
You want to know how it's done? Come and find out some of our amazing secrets[4]! You'll be surprised!

Rides and attractions
Enjoy exciting moments, fast and scary rides! They'll make you scream and they'll make you laugh. See our website for details and new attractions.

Opening times
Summer: Daily 10 am to 8 pm
Winter: Daily 10 am to 6 pm
Now open Christmas Day

Tickets
1 or 2-day tickets
Visit our website for details
Buy online for attractive prices

[1] character ['kærəktə] *Charakter, Wesen* [2] experience [ɪks'pɪəriəns] *Erlebnis, Erfahrung* [3] set [set] *Schauplatz* [4] secret ['siːkrət] *Geheimnis*

4 WORDS Business in California ▸ p. 36

Write the words in the yellow boxes correctly.

gfnamri Farming ______ is very important for Californian business. Because the weather is usually warm and sunny, farmers grow lots of fruit and vegetables. Over 85% of US strawberries come from California, so strawberry pnrdcotiuo ______ is an important tyudirns ______. In Central Valley you see huge lsdiauntri ______ farms. In Napa Valley farmers grow srpgae ______ and make them into enwi ______.

2004 You can buy Californian cspodtru ______ in supermarkets all over the world.

5 WORDS Group words ▸ p. 36

Find and write group words for the following:

1 gardener, farmer, firefighter : jobs ______
2 breakfast, lunch, dinner: ______
3 California, New York, Arizona: ______
4 Spanish, Italian, French: ______
5 Russia, Mexico, Poland: ______
6 Grand Canyon, Yosemite: ______

6 REVISION Verb forms (Past participles) ▸ p. 36

Find the past participles across and down. Then write the three forms of the verbs.

g	r	o	w	n	g	m
s	l	o	s	t	o	a
p	t	f	o	u	n	d
o	a	m	l	u	e	e
k	k	s	d	o	n	e
e	e	s	p	e	n	t
n	n	b	u	i	l	t

grow – grew – grown, ______

______

______

______

______

______

2006

7 The 'Golden State' (Passive – simple present) ▸ p. 36 • GF 2a–c (p. 163)

*Make passive sentences. Exercise **6** will help you.*

California is called ______ (call) the 'Golden State'. Every year it ______ (visit) by millions of tourists from all over the world – and millions of dollars ______ (spend) there on its famous sights and attractions. English and Spanish ______ (speak) because California is the home of lots of Mexican immigrants. California is also the home of the film industry. The name 'Hollywood'

2007 ______ (know) all over the world, just like the films that ______ (make) there.

8 What's made where? (Passive – simple present) ▸ p. 36 • GF 2a–c (p. 163)

Use the information on the map to write sentences in the passive, simple present.

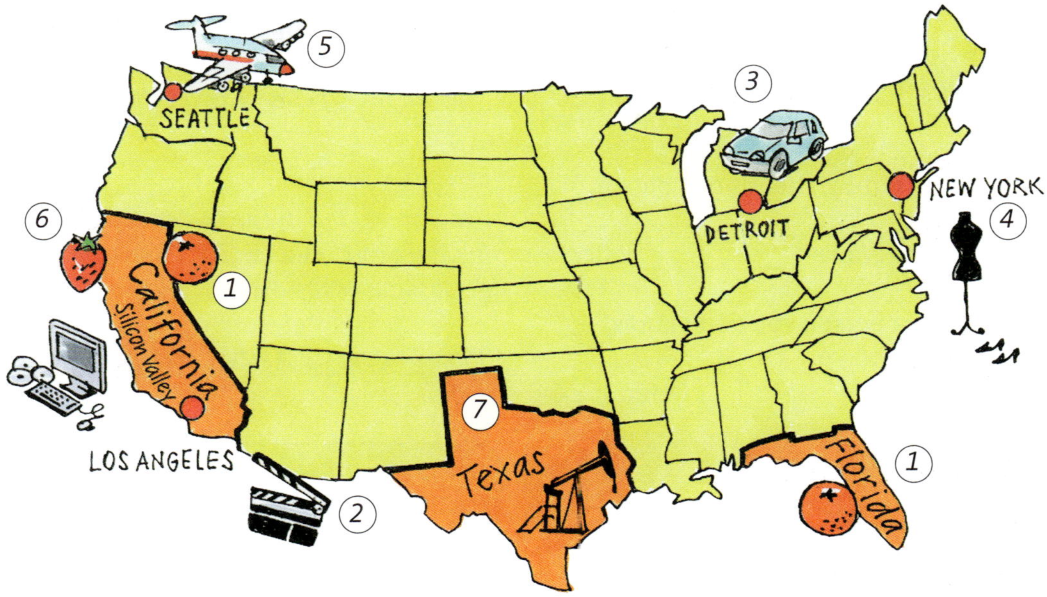

1 grow: *Oranges are grown in California and in Florida.*

2 make: ____________________

3 produce: ____________________

4 design: ____________________

5 build: ____________________

6 grow: ____________________

7 produce: ____________________

Info box

San Francisco is built on 43 hills. It's known as one of the most beautiful cities in the world and it's visited by 17 million tourists each year.

9 WORDS All about ... growing up in two cultures ▸ p. 37

Complete what Luis's friend Lanh says with words from the box.

advantage • *citizen* • cultures • disadvantage • discrimination • ethnic minority • experience • fit in • prejudiced

Hi! My name is Lanh. I'm a US *citizen*, but my family is part of the Vietnamese community[1] here, so we belong to an ____________. For me this isn't a ____________, but some Americans are ____________ against immigrants like us. Some kids in our school have problems with ____________ because they look different. A boy I know from India had a bad ____________ with some white guys. They said he didn't ____________ here and he should go home. I think that growing up in two ____________ is a big ____________. I speak both languages, so I have Vietnamese and US friends – and they all love my cool jokes!

[1] Vietnamese community [viːˌetnəˈmiːz kəˈmjuːnəti] *vietnamesische Gemeinde*

10 WRITING Writing letters

► p. 37 • SF (p. 156)

a) Complete the information about writing letters with:

informal • Yours sincerely • formal
Yours faithfully • Dear Sir or Madam

1 When you write to family, friends or a person you know, you write a/an ____________ letter.

2 When you write to a person you don't know, you write a/an ________________ letter.

3 You begin a formal letter with:

____

4 If you don't know the name, you end a formal letter with:

____

5 If you know the name, you end a formal letter with:

____

b) Luis would like to be on a TV chat show for teenagers. This is his letter to the TV company. Complete it with details about Luis (age, Mexican parents, US citizen, two languages, wants to talk about his experience as a Latino).

____

I am interested in the topic 'Young immigrants in California' and I would like to be in the discussion group on your show on 7th February.

I am 14 years old. My parents ______________

____

____

____

____

____

____

____

Now you

In your exercise book, write a short, formal letter to the editor of a teen magazine. Do you have classmates from other countries? Have you learnt about their cultures from them? Are you growing up in two cultures? Describe the advantages and/or the disadvantages. Read the letters on p. 37 of your student's book for ideas.

I am German but in my class there are lots of students who are not German. I think it is interesting ...

11 When was it done? (Passive – simple past)

► p. 38 • GF 2a–c (p. 163)

First underline the passive forms, then tick (✓) the correct statements and correct the wrong ones. Choose the right answer from the box.

- 1848
- *1769*
- Joseph Strauss
- Hollywood
- Levi Strauss

1 California was discovered in 1910. *Wrong. It was discovered in 1769.*

2 San Francisco was destroyed by an earthquake and fire in 1906. *✓*

3 The first jeans were made by Joseph Strauss. _______________

4 Gold was first found in 1910. _______________

5 The first silent movie[1] was made in Hollywood in 1910. _______________

6 The first talking movies were made in Germany. _______________

2411 7 The Golden Gate Bridge was built by Levi Strauss. _______________

[1] silent movie ['saɪlənt] *Stummfilm*

12 Earthquake country (Passive – simple past)

▸ p. 38 • GF 2a–c (p. 163)

Write the passive form (simple past) of the verbs in the yellow box. Then write the text with the correct passive forms in your exercise book.

Earthquake country: Facts

On April 18, 1906 more than 3,000 people ... in an earthquake and the fires which followed. It ... the Great San Francisco Earthquake. On October 17, 1989 San Francisco's Bay Bridge ... This time the earthquake lasted[1] only 15 seconds, but 3,300 people ... or ... badly.

On January 17, 1994 Los Angeles ... by an earthquake which lasted 40 seconds. 72 people died and hundreds of homes ...

2512

kill: *were killed* ______
call: ______
hit: ______
kill: ______
hurt: ______
hit: ______
destroy: ______

13 Who, what, when? (Passive – simple past)

▸ p. 38 • GF 2a–d (pp. 163–164)

Complete the sentences with the passive form (simple past). Use **by** *if you need it.*

1 

invent[2] – Walt Disney

Mickey Mouse *was invented* ______ by ______

2 

theme park – open

The Universal Studios ______ ______ in 1964.

3 

first – make – Levi Strauss

Jeans ______ ______ ______

4 

San Francisco – destroy – earthquake

______ ______ ______ in 1906.

14 Blue box: little ('wenig') – few ('wenige')

▸ p. 38, p. 182

Underline the correct word/phrase in brackets.

1 Illegal immigrants on industrial farms work for very (little/few) money. They get (less/fewer) money than legal immigrants. Illegal workers get only (a few/the least) dollars an hour.

2 Luis has to go shopping. In the fridge he finds only (a little/a few) milk and (a little/a few) strawberries.

3 Mrs Morales has (a little/a few) jobs. She cleans and cooks in two houses and on (a few/less) days in the week she works as a waitress.

4 Luis saves (a little/a few) pocket money. His brother Diego saves (less/fewer) money, but Luis's friend Lanh saves (few/the least) money – nothing.

2514

[1] last [lɑːst] *dauern* [2] invent, invented, invented [ɪn'vent] *erfinden*

15 A newspaper report (Active and passive) ▸ p. 38 • GF 2a–c (p. 163)

Luis's uncle José has a small café in San Clemente. Last night a thief stole some money. A reporter talked to the police and took some notes. Write full sentences for his report. Use active and passive verbs.

NOTES
- thief entered café through back window
- window opened with a knife
- glass not broken
- thief tried to open safe, but couldn't
- about 300 dollars stolen from kitchen
- left through back door
- teenager in black jeans and black jacket seen
- neighbor called police

1 The thief entered the café through a back window.
2 The window was opened with a knife.
3 ______
4 ______
5 ______
6 ______
7 ______
8 ______

16 LISTENING A dream that came true ▸ p. 38 • SF (p. 148) Track 5

Test

Luis had to find out some facts about the Golden Gate Bridge for homework, but he wrote down some wrong details in his notes. Listen and correct Luis's mistakes.

1 The bridge is ~~0.7~~ miles long. 1.7
2 It takes ~~30~~ minutes to walk across the bridge. ______
3 Joseph Strauss's father was ~~an engineer~~. ______
4 Strauss started to build the bridge in ~~1934~~. ______
5 It was opened on ~~June 20th~~ at 12 o'clock midday. ______
6 It cost 25 million dollars to build. ______
7 It's foggy near the bridge from April to June. ______
8 The bridge is painted gold. ______
9 28 painters work on the bridge. ______
10 Strauss died 10 years after the bridge was finished. ______

17 PRONUNCIATION The same or different? ▸ p. 38 Track 6

Do the underlined parts sound the same? Write Yes or No. Then listen and check.

1 beard – bear	No	5 ethnic – detail	______
2 ruler – movie	Yes	6 work – earthquake	______
3 business – product	______	7 succeed – coffee	______
4 Jewish – attitude	______	8 belong – citizen	______

2617

18 EVERYDAY ENGLISH SPEAKING Living in California ▸ p. 38

Test

Would you like to live in California? Think of at least four good things and four bad things. Brainstorm your ideas and make notes. Then prepare arguments for a class discussion.

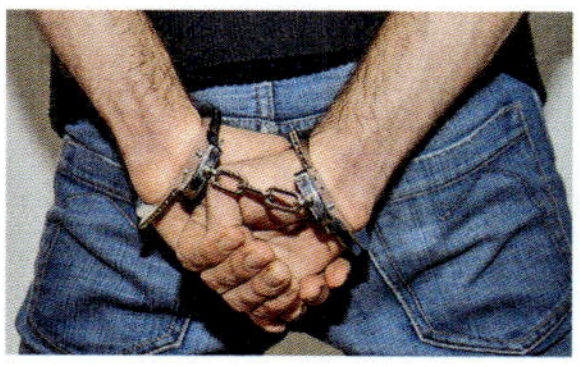

Good things:

weather sunny

Bad things:

earthquakes,

I think there are more advantages than disadvantages ...
First, ... second, ... third, ...
In my opinion ...
I don't agree that ...
2718 Another good/bad thing is (that) ...

Info box

About 40 million people in the US are immigrants, and about 12 million of these are illegal immigrants from Spanish-speaking countries, that's 4% of the population.

19 LISTENING[1] L.A. tours (Recorded messages) ▸ p. 38 • SF (p. 148) Tracks 7, 8

Imagine you are in Los Angeles with your family. You call a tour company and listen to a recorded message. To hear information about the tours you have to press different numbers on your phone.

Test

*a) Listen to **Part 1** (Track 7) on your CD and write the correct number.*

1 If you want to find out about the Disneyland tour, press 2.

2 If you're interested in Beverly Hills and movie stars' homes, press ______.

3 If you want to see L.A. from a helicopter, press ______.

4 If you want to visit Universal Studios, press ______.

5 If you're interested in family tours, press ______.

6 If you want to hear the recorded message again, press ______.

*b) You would like to see where the stars live, so you decide to take the tour that goes to Beverly Hills. Listen to **Part 2** (Track 8) and complete the following notes:*

1 The tour leaves ____________ daily at ______ and ______ pm.

2 The tour lasts[2] ____________ hours.

3 The tour buses pick you up from most L.A. ____________.

4 The tour costs $ ______ for adults and $ ______ for children under ______.

[1] tour guide [gaɪd] *Reiseleiter/in* [2] last [lɑːst] *dauern*

20 Extra Alcatraz (Passive – modals and will-future)

▸ p. 39 • GF 2e (p. 164)

a) Complete the text with these verb forms:

~~had to be closed~~ • will be remembered • should be bought • couldn't be done • can be seen • may be taken

Everybody has heard of Alcatraz or of the gang boss Al Capone, who spent four and a half years of his life there. The prison[1] *had to be closed* in 1963, but now it is a popular tourist attraction. Alcatraz Island ____________ from San Francisco, but you can get there only by ferry. Boat tours ____________ during[2] the day, but in the summer months tickets ____________ at least a week before the tour. Visitors love it! Alcatraz ____________ by Hollywood films like *The Rock*. Some prisoners[3] tried to escape from Alcatraz, but it ____________.

2820

b) Why do you think it was so difficult to escape from Alcatraz? Use the internet, then write some notes in your exercise book. Present your ideas to the class.

21 Extra WORDS California words

▸ p. 39

Write the odd word out. Then write why it's different from the others.

1. strawberries, grapes, oranges, lettuce — *Lettuce.* *The others are kinds of fruit.*
2. immigrant, farmer, firefighter, governor — ____________
3. successful, useful, illegal, minority — ____________
4. San Clemente, San Francisco, Las Vegas, Los Angeles — ____________
5. citizen, member, border, immigrant — ____________
6. sunny, foggy, earthquake, windy — ____________

2821

Fun fact

In 2000, 55 Oscars were stolen on their way to L.A. to the Award[4] Show. 52 were found next to a garbage bin. Willie Fulgear, the man who found them and gave them to the police, got a reward[5] of $50,000 and two tickets to the show. But a few days later his apartment was broken into and the money was stolen! *There are four passive forms here. Can you find them?*

[1] prison ['prɪzn] *Gefängnis* [2] during ['djʊərɪŋ] *während* [3] prisoner ['prɪznə(r)] *Gefangene/r*
[4] award [ə'wɔːd] *Preis* [5] reward [rɪ'wɔːd] *Belohnung*

22 Extra Background File WELCOME TO CALIFORNIA! ▸ pp. 40–41

a) What do you know about California? Tick (✓) A, B or C. You need the letters in brackets in b).

1 California is called ...

A the Sun and Fun State. (S) B the Yellow State. (A) C ✓ the Golden State. (E)

2 'Silicon Valley' is the home of ...

A the movie industry. (E) B the computer industry. (S) C fruit and vegetable farming. (A)

3 Hollywood is part of ...

A San Francisco. (G) B San Diego. (E) C Los Angeles. (N)

4 The first Hollywood movie was made in ...

A 1850. (D) B 1906. (E) C 1910. (I)

5 You can take a ride on a famous cable car in ...

A San Francisco. (Y) B Los Angeles. (R) C San Clemente. (T)

6 What are sequoias?

A A Mexican dish. (N) B A kind of Californian fruit. (I) C Big trees. (D)

b) Now write the letters in brackets from a) in the boxes below. If your answers are correct, the letters make a famous Hollywood name. Here are the question numbers:

6	4	2	3	1	5
				E	

c) What have you learnt from the information on pp. 40–41? Write two interesting facts about each of these topics:

1 Industry in California 2 Hollywood 3 California's National Parks 4 Earthquake country

1 ______________________________

____

____

2 ______________________________

____

3 ______________________________

____

____

4 ______________________________

____

23 WORKING WITH THE TEXT Santa Monica – Episode 1 of a TV series ▸ pp. 49–52

a) Read pp. 49–52 of your student's book again. Which scenes do the pictures show? Write the scene number in the box. Then explain what is happening in the scene.

3 This is the scene where Josh and the others see Jenna with her old car.

She's looking at the engine. Josh is going over to her to help.

This is the last scene. Jenna and Josh are at the Alvarez house.

b) How do you know that Jenna and her family don't have much money?

Jenna needs the job in the café so she's unhappy when she loses it.

c) Why do you think Josh wants to get to know Jenna? Compare Jenna and Josh's friends.

d) Why do you think TV soaps are so popular? Think about where the action usually takes place (for example, in a hospital, a hotel, a big company, rich and poor families, etc.). Think about problems, relationships[1], characters, feelings. Brainstorm and structure your ideas and write about 100 words in your exercise book.

I think TV soaps are so popular because they show everyday problems that ...

[1] relationship [rɪ'leɪʃnʃɪp] *Beziehung*

1 Write the missing words.

1 Wine is made from ______________________.

2 The opposite of 'majority' is ______________________.

3 If you go to another country to work and live without papers, you are an ______________ immigrant.

4 It isn't right to ______________________ against ethnic minorities.

3101 5 The ______________________ of the USA is about 300 milllion.

2 Complete the sentences with passive forms (simple present or simple past).

find • grow • kill • produce

1 Lots of fruit and vegetables ______________________ in California.

2 Californian gold __________ first ______________ in 1848.

3 Computer software ______________________ in Silicon Valley.

3102 4 Last year thousands of animals ______________________ in Californian forest fires.

3 Complete the word families.

	Verb	Noun	Adjective
1	experience		–
2	produce		–
3	–	industry	
4		success	successful
5	discriminate		–
6		prejudice	–

3103

4 STUDY SKILLS What's the difference? Complete with skim or scan.

1 If you want to find the main ideas of a text quickly, you should ______________ the text.

2 You have to ______________ the text if you want to find answers to specific questions.

3104 3 When you ______________ a text you look at bold print, pictures and captions.

18 points

Now you

Write a short essay with the title 'California – a dreamland?'. Do you think it is a dreamland? Say why or why not. Write a paragraph each on industry, tourist activities and problems of the state. Remember to use paragraphs and your writing skills. Write about 100 words in your exercise book.

California is a rich state and there is lots of industry. One of the most important industries is ...
3105 *There are lots of activities for tourists in California. For example, they ...*
3106 *But a rich state also has problems. The weather is good most of the time, but ...*

Jetzt kann ich …	Sehr gut!	OK	Verbessern!
HÖREN: Ich kann …			
… längere Geschichten/Sachtexte verstehen, auch wenn ich einige Wörter nicht kenne.	☐	☐	☐
… aus längeren Listenings Details richtig entnehmen.	☐	☐	☐
… den amerikanischen Akzent heraushören.	☐	☐	☐
… mehrere amerikanische Wörter erkennen und verstehen (z.B. *elevator, gas, cellphone, vacation, sidewalk*).	☐	☐	☐
SPRECHEN: Ich kann …			
… meine Meinung zu Themen im Englischunterricht frei äußern, auch wenn ich kleine Fehler mache.	☐	☐	☐
… über gelesene Texte sprechen und dazu Stellung nehmen.	☐	☐	☐
… in einer amerikanischen Stadt nach dem Weg fragen.	☐	☐	☐
… in einem amerikanischen *deli* ohne Probleme bestellen.	☐	☐	☐
… über Sehenswürdigkeiten in New York und California sprechen.	☐	☐	☐
… über Vor- und Nachteile des Großstadtlebens sprechen.	☐	☐	☐
LESEN: Ich …			
… weiß, wie ich unbekannte Wörter in einem Text erschließen kann.	☐	☐	☐
… kenne die Lesetechniken *skimming* und *scanning* und kann sie anwenden.	☐	☐	☐
… kann längere Sachtexte und Geschichten lesen und verstehen, auch wenn ich einige Wörter nicht kenne.	☐	☐	☐
SCHREIBEN: Ich …			
… kenne die Texttypen *diary, essay, presentation, blog, e-mail* und *postcard* und kann sie stilistisch voneinander unterscheiden.	☐	☐	☐
… kann die britische und die amerikanische Schreibweise einiger Wörter unterscheiden (z.B. BE: *colour, centre*; AE: *color, center*).	☐	☐	☐
… kann Fragen zu Texten der Units 1 und 2 schriftlich beantworten.	☐	☐	☐
… kann meine Sätze mit *adjectives, adverbs, time phrases* und *linking words* verbinden und ausbauen, um sie sprachlich interessanter zu gestalten.	☐	☐	☐
LAND UND LEUTE: Ich …			
… kenne einige berühmte Sehenswürdigkeiten in New York und Kalifornien (z.B. *Empire State Building, Ellis Island, the Golden Gate Bridge, Silicon Valley*).	☐	☐	☐
… könnte mich in Manhattan zurechtfinden. Mehrere Straßennamen sind mir geläufig (z.B. *Fifth Avenue, Broadway*).	☐	☐	☐
… weiß, dass New York 5 Bezirke hat: *Manhattan, Queens, Brooklyn, the Bronx, Staten Island.*	☐	☐	☐
… habe einiges über die Situation von Immigranten in Kalifornien (*Mexicans*) gelernt.	☐	☐	☐
… weiß einiges über die Geschichte, den Handel und die Industrie in Kalifornien (z.B. Obst- und Weinanbau, Filme, Tourismus, Computer).	☐	☐	☐

Jetzt kann ich ...

	Sehr gut!	OK	Verbessern!
GRAMMATIKVERSTÄNDNIS: Ich kann ...			
... das Gerundium (*gerund*) richtig bilden und als Subjekt und als Objekt eines Satzes einsetzen (z.B. *Flying is great. / I love flying.*).	☐	☐	☐
... das Gerundium nach gewissen Verben (z.B. *enjoy, finish, practise*) und nach Präpositionen richtig einsetzen (z.B. *I enjoy reading. / I'm interested in learning languages.*).	☐	☐	☐
... den Unterschied zwischen einem Aktiv- und einem Passivsatz erkennen und das Passiv im *simple present* und im *simple past* richtig bilden (z.B. *Strawberries are grown in California. Last year 700,000 tons were produced.*).	☐	☐	☐
... das Passiv mit '*by*' verwenden, wenn ich den 'Täter' oder 'Verursacher' der Handlung nennen will (z.B. *The Golden Gate Bridge was built by Joseph Strauss.*).	☐	☐	☐
VOKABELVERSTÄNDNIS: Ich kann ...			
... amerikanische Wörter von britischen unterscheiden (z.B. BE: *rubbish, biscuit;* AE: *garbage, cookie*).	☐	☐	☐
... amerikanische Wörter/Wendungen für eine Wegbeschreibung richtig verwenden (z.B. *block, downtown, 34th and Broadway*).	☐	☐	☐
... Wörter, die ethnische Minderheiten und ihre Probleme beschreiben, richtig anwenden (z.B. *ethnic, minority, discrimination, prejudice, illegal*).	☐	☐	☐
SKILLS – LERNEN UND ARBEITEN: Ich ...			
... kenne Arbeitstechniken, die mir helfen, unbekannte Wörter in einem Text ohne Wörterbuch zu erschließen (z.B. Bilder, Kontext, Wortfamilien).	☐	☐	☐
... kann Lesetechniken wie *skimming* und *scanning* erfolgreich anwenden.	☐	☐	☐
... kann Gesprochenes auf Englisch und Deutsch sinngemäß weitergeben (*mediation*), z.B. bei der Einholung von Informationen.	☐	☐	☐

WAS ICH FÜR MEIN ENGLISCHLERNEN GETAN HABE: Ich habe ...	häufig	manchmal	nie
... im Englischunterricht gut aufgepasst und aktiv mitgearbeitet.	☐	☐	☐
... gelernte Arbeitstechniken bewusst eingesetzt.	☐	☐	☐
... die Aufgaben im Grammar File und Skills File in meinem Buch bearbeitet.	☐	☐	☐

WIE ICH MICH VERBESSERN KÖNNTE: Ich könnte ...

- ... Vokabel- und Grammatikkenntnisse regelmäßig auffrischen. ☐
- ... ein deutsch-englisches Wörterbuch häufiger verwenden. ☐
- ... ausgewählte Workbook-Übungen der Bände 2 und 3 noch einmal bearbeiten. ☐
- ... mir häufiger Texte von meiner CD anhören, um mich an die Aussprache und Betonung zu gewöhnen. ☐
- ... DVDs auf Englisch anschauen. ☐
- ... englischsprachige Zeitschriften oder Websites lesen. ☐

Unit 3 Hermann says 'Willkommen'

1 About Hermann

▸ pp. 54–55

Test

a) What do you know about Missouri, Hermann and the Schmidts? Read pp. 54–55 of your student's book again. Have you listened to 'Arriving in Hermann' in your student's book? If yes, are the statements right or wrong? Mark a number.

	Right	Wrong
1 Hermann was founded in 1837.	15	45
2 The journey by car from St. Louis to Hermann only takes half an hour.	65	35
3 Hermann is on the Missouri River.	74	38
4 Lots of houses were built by Germans in the 17th century.	36	26
5 There aren't many restaurants in Hermann.	75	90
6 There's only one traffic light in Hermann.	95	44
7 Not many tourists visit Hermann.	22	30
8 Maifest and Oktoberfest are very popular festivals in Hermann.	35	22

3401

Now add together the numbers that are marked: ________.

If your answers are correct, you have written the number of students at Hermann High School. Check your answer on p. 54 of your student's book.

***b)** Look at the photos of Hermann on pp. 54–55. Write a description of the town in 60–80 words.*

Hermann is a small town in the state of Missouri. There isn't much traffic

____

____

____

____

____

***c)** Compare Hermann High School (photo E, p. 54 in your student's book) with your school. Is your school modern too? Has your school got 400 students or more? Has your school got a running track, a football pitch and equipment for athletics? Has your school got a large car park? Write 80–100 words in your exercise book. Remember to structure your ideas and use your writing skills.*

Our school is modern too. / Our school isn't as modern as … Our school looks quite different from …

2 EVERYDAY ENGLISH WRITING A letter (Letter for information) ▸ p. 55 • SF (p. 156)

Test

*Imagine that you need information about US schools for a project. Write a letter to Jake Kruger and ask him about schools in Hermann. Start and finish your letter correctly. Look at the letter in exercise **2** on p. 62 of your student's book for help.*

Tell him:
- who you are, where you are from
- why you are writing
- where you go to school
- how old you are, what year you are in

You could ask him about these things:
- the school day
- homework, projects
- school subjects
- clubs and school holidays

(your address) ____________________

____

(today's date) ____________________

Dear Jake,

____

____

____

____

____

____

____

____

3 WORDS Blue box: Facts about Hermann ▸ p. 55, p. 187 Track 9

Say and write the numbers. Then listen and check.

You see:	You say:
1 Hermann was founded in **1837**.	eighteen (hundred and) thirty-seven
2 Hermann has a population of about **2,674**.	
3 The town has an area of **6.4 sq km**.	
4 **54.4%** of the population comes from German families.	
5 In the 9th grade at Hermann High there are **112** students.	
6 At Hermann High **52%** of the students are girls.	
7 In winter, temperatures might drop to **– 12° C**.	

4 WORDS All about … American schools ▸ p. 56

a) Draw lines to match the information in the boxes.

US schools

Ages 6–11	High School	Grades 1–5
Ages 11–14	Elementary School	Grades 9–12
Ages 14–18	Middle School	Grades 6–8

US grades

A	below average
B	failure
C	excellent
D	good
F	average

b) If you went to school in the US, which kind of school and which grade would you be in?

I think I'd be in ________________________ in grade ____

I think my brother/sister would be in __________

c) If you went to school in the US, what grades would you have in English, Maths, Art, etc.?

I think I'd have a ____

5 WORDS School words: BE and AE ▸ p. 56

a) Write the words in the correct lists.

timetable • *Schulstunde* • vacation • grade • bulletin board • Jahrgangsstufe • *period* • Anschlagtafel • year • schedule • holiday(s) • Ferien • *lesson* • notice board • Stundenplan

1	*Schulstunde*	*period*	*lesson*
2			
3			
4			
5			

3605

b) Where are the two students from? The USA or the UK? First underline the AE und BE words.

I'm in year 9. Our timetable is good this year. I've just read our sports results on the notice board. My next lesson is PE in the gym.

My schedule is OK and my grades aren't too bad, but I'm looking forward to the summer vacation.

Kate is from the __________ .   Josh is from the __________ .

Info box

Missouri …

- is the birthplace of 33rd US President Harry S. Truman, Jesse James (outlaw[1]) and Mark Twain, writer of *Tom Sawyer and The Adventures of Huckleberry Finn*,
- is the birthplace of peanut[2] butter and the ice cream cone[3].

[1] outlaw ['aʊtlɔː] *Bandit*   [2] peanut ['piːnʌt] *Erdnuss*   [3] cone [kəʊn] *Spitztüte*

6 EVERYDAY ENGLISH SPEAKING A talk about schools ▸ p. 57

Test

Timo has to tell his new class about school in Germany. He wants to talk about the main differences between US and German schools. Here are his notes:

	In Germany ...	In the USA ...
1 school grades:	• 1–6	• A–F
2 school day:	• not usually afternoon	• until 3 pm every day
3 lunch:	• usually no lunch	• hot lunch at school
4 classrooms:	• students change only for some subjects	• different rooms for different subjects, students change for each period
5 vacation:	• 6 weeks in summer	• 3 months in summer
6 extracurriculars:	• not many	• a lot – very important

Prepare a talk from Timo's notes and practise it for class.

German schools are different from US schools in a few ways. For example, school grades are different, the school day and extracurricular activities. First I want to talk about ...

Now you

What do you think is good about US schools? Say why. What do you like better at your German school? Say why. Write two paragraphs in your exercise book.

Some things about US schools are really good. For example, the long summer holidays and ...

7 An hour, some time (Countable/uncountable nouns) ▸ p. 57 • GF 3 (p. 165)

*Which words go with **a/an**? Which go with **some**? Join them. Then highlight the words that go with **a/an** with yellow and the the words that go with **some** with blue.*

information | job | meal | news

hour — a / an | some — time

bottle | work

event | food | gold | piece

3707

8 A sandwich and some milk (countable/ uncountable nouns) ▸ p. 57 • GF 3 (p. 165)

*Complete the dialogue with **a/an** or **some**.*

Mom Time to go, Jake. The school bus will be here soon.

Jake OK. I'll just have __a__ sandwich and __some__ milk for breakfast if there's ________ white bread. I still have ________ homework to do, but it's just reading.

Mom I thought you had ________ essay for American History, and you have ________ homework for Science too.

Jake Not for today, Mom. I need ________ information for the essay, and maybe ________ help from Dad.

Mom Well, here's ________ money for a hot lunch. And how about ________ fruit – ________ apple or ________ grapes?

Jake Or how about ________ big piece of chocolate cake?

9 Jake hasn't got much pocket money (Countable/uncountable nouns) ▸ p. 57 • GF 3 (p. 165)

Complete the text with: some • a • much • many

Jake is planning a German barbecue[1] for Timo and Anna and his friends. There are __some__ things to decide. How ________ kids should he invite? How ________ food should he buy? Maybe his mom will give him ________ help with this. For a German barbecue he needs ________ sausages, but how ________ sausages should he buy? ________ kilo? And of course there must be ________ potato salad, but how ________ should he make? And there must be ________ drinks: ________ cola ________ ice-tea. How ________ bottles should he buy? Jake hasn't got ________ pocket money, but maybe his parents will give him ________ extra pocket money. And, very important for a good party: ________ great music and ________ good DJ.

3809

10 School is different in Hermann (Definite article) ▸ p. 58 • GF 4 (p. 166)

Add the where you need it.

1 Timo thought that ______ school in Hermann would be the same as school in Bad Arolsen, but some things are different. ______ school that he goes to is a high school.

2 ______ subjects that Timo has in Hermann are not the same as ______ subjects he had in Bad Arolsen.

3 Timo is usually quite good at ______ homework, but the couldn't do ______ homework he got in American History and Government.

4 ______ German sports teams don't have cheerleaders, but ______ sports teams at Hermann High all have cheerleaders.

3810

11 WORDS Word building (Nouns from verbs and adjectives) ▸ p. 58

a) Which verb or adjective do these nouns come from? If you are not sure, use your Dictionary in your student's book (pp. 194–224).

activity – __active__	discrimination – ________	discussion – ________
reality – ________	happiness – ________	installation – ________
invitation – ________	madness – ________	mediation – ________
nationality – ________	presentation – ________	revision – ________

b) Now complete the sentences with a noun from a).

1 There's a Science test next week, so the students have to do some ________ at the weekend.

2 Timo thinks that showing hogs is a very strange ________, but he's going to join the FFA.

3 At the FFA meeting there was a good ________ on the Missouri wine industry.

3811

4 Jake is good with computers. He helped Anna with the ________ of lots of programmes.

[1] barbecue ['bɑːbɪkjuː] *Grillparty*

12 READING COURSE
Part 3: US students and sport (Finding the main ideas of a text)

▸ p. 58 • SF (p. 151)

a) Read the text carefully.

(1) US teenagers do not do enough sport to keep fit and healthy. As children grow older, they become less and less active, and by 12th grade physical[1] activity has reached[2] its lowest level[3]. ← **Topic**

(2) Experts agree that students in grades 9–12 spend too much time sitting and spend too little time on physical activities For example, 35% of US high school students do not take part in sports regularly[4]. This fact alone can be the reason for serious health problems when they're adults. ← **Main idea** ← **Example/Reason**

(3) One problem is that our modern lifestyle with its electronic media means that teenagers spend many hours on activities where they just sit. These activities are, for example, watching TV or DVDs, playing video and computer games or using computer and cellphones to contact friends. Studies[5] have shown that 17% of young people in the US watch TV for more than 5 hours a day.

(4) How students get to school is another reason for physical inactivity[6]. National transportation studies say that for safety reasons most students are taken to school by bus or by car, even if school is only one mile or less away from home. Older students drive to school in their own cars, so walking or cycling to school is something that most high school students just do not do.

(5) What can be done to change the attitude of teenagers to sport and physical activities? In many parts of the USA communities and local[7] government work together to offer physical activity programs for young people. But physical activity is voluntary[8], so students will join programs only if they are enjoyable, close to home and free.

b) *Read the text paragraph by paragraph. Find and mark the sentence in each paragraph that gives you the main idea.*

c) *Find the examples to the main ideas in each paragraph and mark them. Use a different colour.*

d) *Which of the statements below (A–E) goes with which paragraph (1–5)?*

A: Physical activity programs of local communities have to be fun. (Paragraph ______)

B: Most high school students do not walk or cycle to school. (Paragraph ______)

C: Our modern lifestyle makes young people physically inactive. (Paragraph ______)

D: US high school students do not spend enough time doing sports. (Paragraph ______)

E: Experts say that students in grades 9–12 sit too much in their free time. (Paragraph ______)

e) **Extra** *What's the general attitude to sports and health in your school year? Do you and your friends take part in physical activities (running, cycling, swimming, etc.) in your free time? Or do you spend more time with electronic media? Which? Write a short text in your exercise book.*

[1] physical ['fɪzɪkl] *körperlich* [2] reach [riːtʃ] *erreichen* [3] lowest level ['ləʊɪst 'levl] *niedrigste Stufe*
[4] regularly ['regjələli] *regelmäßig* [5] studies ['stʌdiːz] *Studien* [6] inactivity [ˌɪnæk'tɪvəti] *Untätigkeit*
[7] local ['ləʊkl] *örtlich, heimisch* [8] voluntary ['vɒləntri] *freiwillig*

13 WORDS Food ▸ p. 58

a) Put the food and drink words in the list where they fit best: breakfast, lunch/dinner or snacks.

beans • *beef* • biscuits • *bread* • carrots • cheese • chicken • chocolate • coffee • cornflakes • crisps • curry • eggs • fish • fruit • fruit juice • hamburgers • ice cream • lamb • marmalade • milk • muesli • nuts • pasta • peas • pork • potatoes • rice • rolls • sausages • soft drinks • soup • steak • tea • toast • turkey

breakfast	lunch/dinner	snacks

bread,	*beans, beef,*	

b) What's your favourite breakfast? What's your favourite snack? Write two paragraphs in your exercise book.

My favourite breakfast is cornflakes with milk, then brown bread with cheese ...

14 LISTENING After the Health class ▸ p. 58 • SF (p. 148) Track 10

After school three students from Jake's class are talking about food. Listen and tick (✓) the correct box. Who ...?

	Mike	Donna	Dylan
1 enjoyed learning about the food pyramid?		✓	
2 joked about the food pyramid?			
3 likes healthy food best?			
4 gets angry?			
5 thinks chocolate is good for you?			
6 really likes burgers with fries and ketchup?			
7 suddenly feels hungry?			
8 suggests[1] a pizza place?			
9 asks Donna to join them?			
10 suggests a pizza to go?			
11 wants to eat a pizza outside?			
12 is going to have a party next Saturday?			

Info box

Quick calorie check:	kcal
1 hamburger	254
1 cheeseburger	379
1 serving[2] French fries	294
1 slice[3] pizza Margherita	171
1 can[4] cola (0,33l)	155

To burn the calories in one can of cola you have to walk for 23 minutes!

[1] suggest [sə'dʒest] *vorschlagen* [2] serving ['sɜːvɪŋ] *Portion* [3] slice [slaɪs] *Scheibe* [4] can *Dose*

15 Jake's bad day (Past perfect)

▸ p. 59 • GF 5 (p. 167)

a) Match the sentence halves.

1 When Jake got up, he was tired
2 After he had got ready for school,
3 But the school bus had already left
4 When he arrived at school,
5 Jake's English teacher wasn't very happy

because Jake had come too late to his lesson.
he left home in a hurry.
the first lesson had already started.
because he had gone to bed too late.
when he got to the bus stop.

4115

b) Now write the missing verbs in the past perfect.

1 Jake was hungry in the first lesson because he ____________ (not have) time for breakfast.

2 The history teacher got angry with him after she ____________ (tell) him to stop talking twice.

3 The history teacher was also angry with him because he ____________ (not do) his homework.

Just for fun

Boy: Yesterday my teacher punished[1] me for something that I hadn't done.
Dad: Really? That wasn't fair. What was it that you hadn't done?
Boy: My English essay.

16 Jake's barbecue (Simple past or past perfect)

▸ p. 59 • GF 5 (p. 167)

a) Choose the correct verb form from the brackets.

1 When the guests arrived, Jake *had prepared* (prepared/had prepared) the food.

2 Timo wanted to help, but Jake ____________ (had already done/did) most of the work.

3 Jake didn't start the barbecue until most of the guests ____________ (arrived/had arrived).

4 Two kids came late because they ____________ (forgot/had forgotten) their presents for Jake.

b) Now write the correct verb form. Simple past or past perfect?

1 After the kids ____________ (eat) all the food, they ____________ (dance) and had lots of fun.

2 Jake ________ (go) to the supermarket to get more cola, but it ____________ (already close).

3 The music ____________ (be) great because Jake ____________ (find) a fantastic DJ.

4116 4 Anna ____________ (not meet) most of the kids before, so she ________ (make) lots of new friends.

17 WORDS Write the opposites

▸ p. 59

soft	– *hard*	comfortable	– ________	fat	– ________
majority	– ________	a lot	– ________	the most	– ________
appear	– ________	advantage	– ________	above	– ________
legal	– ________	dead	– ________	possible	– ________

4117

[1] punish ['pʌnɪʃ] *bestrafen*

18 STUDY SKILLS Summarizing texts: Hermann Maifest ▸ p. 59 • SF (p. 157)

Test

a) Read the story about Dylan and his friends at Maifest in Hermann. Watch for the main events.

It was the third weekend in May, Maifest time. The whole of Hermann was excited. The town was alive with attractions, shows, singing and dancing.

'Now be sure to have a good time, you guys, and take care[1] of Bobby, Dylan. Don't lose him. There will be so many visitors in town this weekend,' said Mrs Kaiser as Dylan, Donna and Mike left for the Maifest. The three students were part of the High School Band, so they were already dressed in their German costumes[2]. Dylan even had a solo part on his trumpet. Nobody could play the trumpet like Dylan.

'I just love Maifest,' Donna said as they walked through the busy streets in the sunshine. 'Why can't we have Maifest every weekend? There's so much to see, and lots of cute[3] guys come from other high schools!'

'Girls!' said Dylan, as they turned into Schiller Street. They stopped to listen to the Spitzbaum German Band, then they looked at the food stalls[4] and the big market at Volksplatz. Bobby loved the puppet[5] show and the mini train ride. Then they met more friends, laughed and joked and cheered.

An hour later Dylan looked at his watch. It would soon be time to go to the Festhalle for their concert.
'I have to take Bobby home first, then I'll meet you guys in the park, OK? Come on, Bobby, we have to go home now. Bobby? Bobby? Where is he? Where's Bobby?' Bobby wasn't there ...

Dylan, Donna and the others looked everywhere, but Bobby was nowhere. They asked lots of people on the streets, but nobody had seen him. Maifest was no fun any more. Dylan was scared, really scared. Had someone taken his little brother?

'Dylan, I think you should call your mom,' said Donna nervously.
'But Mom will kill me, Donna. She told me to look after Bobby – but I didn't. I was just having fun with you guys. And what about our concert? I have to play my trumpet solo in ten minutes! Bobby must be somewhere. We just have to look everywhere again – fast.'

'Hey, look! Here comes the parade[6]! Look at the costumes! It's just like the very first Maifest in the 1870s,' said Mike, but nobody was listening ...

'Call your mom, Dylan. You have to call her,' said Donna again. Nervously, Dylan took his cellphone out of his pocket ...

'Hey, guys, look at the old German cars in the parade, and the old fire truck[7] and ... Dylan, look who's sitting in the old fire truck with my dad, wearing a fire helmet – it's Bobby!' said Donna.

'Oh, Mom! Hi, Mom! Er ... it's Dylan. I just wanted to tell you that we're having a great time – Bobby too.'

b) Go through each paragraph and underline the important facts (main events). Think about how you can shorten detailed information. Then write notes in your exercise book.

c) Use your notes to write a summary of the story in your own words. Remember to leave out direct speech, details and long description, and use the simple present.

The story is about Dylan, a student from Hermann High School, who goes to Maifest with his friends and his little brother. First they ...

[1] take care [keə] *aufpassen* [2] costume ['kɒstjuːm] *Kostüm* [3] cute [kjuːt] *süß, niedlich* [4] stall [stɔːl] *Stand* [5] puppet ['pʌpɪt] *Puppe, Marionette* [6] parade [pə'reɪd] *Parade* [7] fire truck [trʌk] *Feuerwehrauto*

19 Extra Background File GOING WEST ▸ pp. 60–61

Test

a) Read the statements. Are they right or wrong? Mark a letter.

	Statement	Right	Wrong
1	Hermann was founded in 1837.	I	S
2	When World War I started, the people of Hermann stopped speaking German.	N	T
3	The first states of the United States were in the West.	L	D
4	Missouri became a state in 1840.	O	E
5	After 1848 Missouri became the 'Gateway to the West'.	P	I
6	Wagon trains were the safest way to travel to the West.	E	C
7	People bought all the things they needed for the long journey in Hermann.	B	N
8	More than half a million people travelled west with the wagon trains.	D	P
9	The first railway across the country was finished in 1869.	E	A
10	About ten per cent of the people were killed by wild animals or Native Americans.	S	N
11	In the beginning, the meetings between Europeans and the Native Americans were not peaceful.	R	C
12	Today only 1.5% of the US population are Native Americans.	E	T

If your answers are correct, the letters give you the name of a town in Missouri: ______________________

b) Read pp. 60–61 in your student's book again, then answer the questions in one or two sentences each.

1 **A:** Why was the town of Hermann founded?

____

____

____

2 **B:** Why did so many people want to go west in the years after 1848? Give two reasons.

____

____

____

3 **C:** Why was the journey west so hard?

____

____

____

4 **D:** What happened to the Native Americans when the settlers went west?

____

____

____

20 WORKING WITH THE TEXT Angus Bethune's moment ▸ pp. 68–70

a) *Finish the statements with information from the story.*

1 The story is about a boy called Angus who *has problems at school because he is fat.*

2 Angus is elected Winter Ball King, but ______

3 Angus was elected because Melissa's boyfriend, Rick, ______

4 Angus is OK on the dance floor because ______

5 Melissa tells Angus that ______

6 After the first dance ______

7 When Angus and Melissa dance the second time, ______

8 At the end Rick is angry and ______

9 But Angus is happy because ______

b) *Choose a picture and describe what is happening. Write in your exercise book.*

I think Picture 1 shows the scene where ...

c) *Do you like the ending? Why or why not? Write a paragraph in your exercise book.*

Ideas: funny • fantastic • surprising • clever • unrealistic • sad • silly

I like the ending. In my opinion it's ... because ... I don't think the ending is very realistic because ...

d) **Extra** *What do you think is more important:*
1) looking good and acting cool (like Rick) or 2) being a really nice person (like Angus)?
What are the advantages and disadvantages of both? Write about 100 words in your exercise book.

1 Write the missing words.

1 The ______________________________ around Hermann is very pretty, green and hilly.

2 Good food and exercise are important for your ______________________.

3 Soda _________________________ lots of sugar.

4 Don't eat so much white bread. Eat _______________________ bread!

4501 *5* US school grade C means '________________________'.

2 Add **the** where you need it.

1 Jake: I need some money for the weekend. I'm visiting a friend in St. Louis.

The problem is, I've already spent ____________ money I got for my birthday.

Timo: I know what you mean. _______ money is only a problem when you don't have any.

2 _______ tourists always come to Hermann at Maifest and Oktoberfest time. Lots of them are from

4502 Germany. __________ tourists who took part in the Maifest parade were from Rüdesheim.

3 Put in a/an, some, much or many.

1 Timo hasn't got ___________ homework today, but he needs _____________ information about

Hermann's wineries for _____________ essay.

2 He hasn't found _______________ facts in his school books, but there's still _____________ time

4503 to ask questions at the wineries.

4 Summarizing texts: Find and tick (✓) the four correct statements.

To write a good summary you should ...

- give only the most important information from the original text. _____
- tell the reader what the text or story is about in the first few sentences . _____
- explain **who** does **what**, **where**, **when** and **why**. _____
- give lots of details. _____
- use the simple present and your own words. _____
- 4504 use lots of adjectives for description and comparisons. _____

18 points

Now you

4505 4506 *Write a short essay with the title 'US and German schools: a comparison'. Use the information in your student's book and exercises 4–6 of this unit in your workbook. Remember your writing skills. Write about 120 words.*

Here are some exercises that will help you with your practice test 2.

1 WORDS Holiday words ▸ pp. 72–73

a) Match the words in the box to the kind of holiday. Make three lists.

ball games • bay • *cabin* • camping gear • canyon • caravan • *castle* • cathedral • church • column • cows • downtown • hike • lake • market • mosque • museum • ocean • palace • parliament • path • rocks • rucksack • sea • sunglasses • surfboard • swimmer • swimming trunks • swimsuit • tent • ticket office • tour guide • towel • tower • valley • views • volleyball • walking shoes

A mountain holiday: *cabin,* ______________________

____

A beach holiday: *ball games,* ______________________

____

A sightseeing holiday: *castle,* ______________________

____

b) Which kind of holiday from a) do you like best? Write your reasons in a paragraph.

I like ______ *holidays best because* ______________________

____

____

____

____

2 Going on holiday (Mixed prepositions) ▸ pp. 72–73

Complete with the correct prepositions:

on • of • to • in • at • by

1 We usually go *on* holiday ______ Easter or ______ summer.

2 When you flew ______ New York, did you land ______ JFK? It's ______ Queens, isn't it?

3 When it's 10 o'clock ______ the morning in New York, it's 4 o'clock ______ the afternoon in Germany.

4 I've taken a really good photo ______ the Golden Gate Bridge. I'll show it ______ you tomorrow.

5 My dad doesn't like flying. He goes everywhere ______ train or car.

6 My mum doesn't like sitting ______ a beach all day. She likes going ______ boat trips or bus tours.

3 My dream holiday (Conditional sentences 2) ▸ pp. 72–73

Where would you spend your US dream holiday – if you could? Grand Canyon, New York, San Francisco, Los Angeles, Las Vegas, Miami, Washington? Choose a place. If you went there, what would/could you do? Write a paragraph. You have to use conditional sentences 2 at least twice in your text.

I would spend my US dream holiday in ... if I could. I would go to ... If I went there, I could ...

____

____

____

____

____

____

4 SPEAKING Making suggestions, agreeing or disagreeing ▸ pp. 72–73

a) *How would you make a suggestion? How would you agree or disagree with a suggestion? Match.*

Making suggestions	Yes, let's do that.
Agreeing	We could go/watch ...
Disagreeing	I'm not sure if I like that idea.
	That's a good/great... idea.
	What about going/watching ... ?
	I don't really want to do that.
	Let's go/watch/ ...

b) *Look at the photos of the beach and the aqua park. A friend suggests going to one of these places. What would you say? Give your reasons. Write a short dialogue in your exercise book.*

Unit 4 Atlanta rising

1 Atlanta, Georgia ▸ pp. 76–77

Test

a) Are the statements below right or wrong? Read pp. 76–77 of your student's book again. Have you listened to 'An Atlanta timeline' in your student's book? If yes, mark a letter.

	Right	Wrong
1 Atlanta is the capital of Alabama.	A	O
2 Atlanta was founded in 1847.	B	R
3 Black slaves from Africa worked on the cotton plantations in the South.	C	K
4 The American Civil War began in 1865.	A	L
5 In 1864 Atlanta was burned down.	L	R
6 The Southern states won the Civil War.	S	N
7 The chemist Pemberton invented[1] a drink which is known all over the world.	N	S
8 Martin Luther King was a Civil Rights leader.	I	A
9 CNN, the world's first 24-hour news station, started in Atlanta in 1980.	T	P
10 Shirley Franklin was elected Atlanta's first black woman mayor in 1999.	S	L
11 Today 61% of Atlanta's population is black.	I	S

4801

Put the letters that are marked in the correct order to make the name of the man who opened the Atlanta Olympic Games.

The name of the man is ______________________.

b) What do you remember about the events on the Atlanta timeline from 1968–2002? In your exercise book, describe each event in one or two sentences.

In 1968 the civil rights leader Martin Luther King was shot and killed. In 1980 ...

2 Blue box: German 'während' ▸ pp. 76–77, p. 189

*Complete the sentences with **during** or **while**.*

1 Before the American Civil War white plantation owners[2] got rich ____________ their black slaves had a terrible life.

2 ________________ the Civil War Atlanta was burned down.

3 Over 620,000 Americans were killed ________________ the years 1861 to 1865.

4 In 1884, __________ Pemberton was trying to help people feel better, he invented a world-famous drink.

4802

5 ________________ the years 1955 to 1968 King worked very hard for the rights of African Americans.

Fun fact

Georgia is the USA's top producer of the '3 Ps' – peanuts[3], pecans[4] and peaches[5].

[1] invent [ɪn'vent] *erfinden* [2] owner ['əʊnə(r)] *Besitzer/in* [3] peanut [piːnʌt] *Erdnuss* [4] pecan ['piːkən, AE: pɪ'kɑːn] *Pekannuss* [5] peach [piːtʃ] *Pfirsich*

3 WORDS All about ... television ▸ p. 78

a) Match the words and the definitions.

1 news	• a programme which gives information about events or topics
2 documentary	• the time when most people watch TV in the evening
3 TV listings	• a programme that is shown on TV for a second or third time
4 prime time	• a programme where people play against each other to win
5 rerun/repeat	• a programme that reports true events of the day
6 competition	• information about times of TV programmes for the week

4903

b) Now explain these words and complete the sentences.

1 A newsreader is someone ____________________

2 A comedy is a ____________________

3 A viewer ____________________

4 A crime series ____________________

c) **Extra** *Which type of programmes do you watch most? Choose two or three types from the box and give an example of each from German TV. Say why you like the programmes that you watch. Write in your exercise book.*

crime series • sports programmes • game shows
quiz shows • documentaries • news programmes • comedy series
reality shows • chat shows • cartoons • action films
soaps • music programmes

Ideas: *make you laugh* • *give you lots of information* • *interesting* • *funny* • *exciting* • *scary*

4 WORDS Watching TV ▸ p. 78

Write the missing words in the puzzle to find the word down.

1 You check the TV ... to see what's on TV.
2 People who watch TV are called ...
3 Your ... control has buttons for everything.
4 If a programme is boring, you can ... channels.
5 Have you got cable TV or ... TV?
6 It's too loud. Can you turn the ... down, please?
7 How many ... can you receive? – Hundreds!
4904
8 It would be nice to have a big flat ... on the wall.

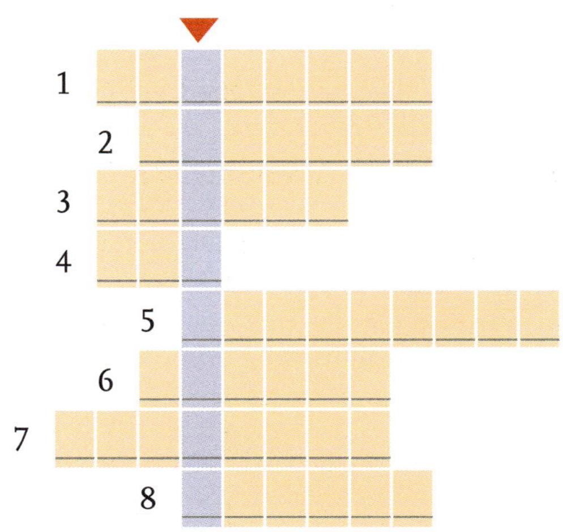

▶ *If your answers are correct, you have written the name of a very popular US TV series:*

The ____________________ .

5 EVERYDAY ENGLISH SPEAKING Talking about soap operas ▸ p. 78 Track 11

Test

Listen to the dialogue between Katie and her brother Mason. They have different opinions of TV soap operas. What do you think? Do you agree with Katie or with Mason? Make notes and prepare your arguments ***for*** *or* ***against*** *soaps for a two-minute talk in class. The words and phrases below will help you.*

I (don't) agree with … • In my opinion … • My opinion is that … • I think … • how people live
you can learn sth. • show different lifestyles • actors • characters • music • problems
everyday situations • events • modern • brilliant • cool • interesting • realistic
terrible • stupid • silly • boring • (un)realistic • uncool • awful

NOTES: For/Against soap operas

Katie's arguments:

Mason's arguments:

Your opinion:

5005

6 EVERYDAY ENGLISH WRITING

My favourite TV programme ▸ p. 78 • SF (pp. 154–155)

Test

Write an e-mail to a friend about your favourite TV programme (show, series, etc.). First make notes which answer these questions:

- When is it on (day and time)?
- How often is it on?
- Which channel is it on?
- What kind of programme is it (music programme, crime series, soap opera, etc.)?
- Who is in it (presenter, actors, etc.)?
- If there is a story, what is it about ?
- Why do you like the programme?
- Do you sometimes record it?
- Do your friends/your family like it too?

Write the e-mail in your exercise book. The ideas in the box will help you:

Dear …
My favourite programme was on TV again yesterday/last night.
I must tell you about it! It's called … and it's on at … pm every … It's on channel … and it lasts for … It's about …
It's really interesting/exciting/scary …
It's my favourite programme because …

7 TYCTWD ▸ p. 79

a) Tick (✓) the correct answer, A, B or C. You need the letters in brackets in part b).

1 TYCTWD takes place ...

A twice a year. (A) B on the fourth Thursday in April. (W) C on the fourth Tuesday in April. (C)

2 Who takes part in TYCTWD?

A All schools and all companies. (G) B All schools and some companies. (O)

C Not all companies or schools. (T)

3 How many students usually take part in TYCTWD?

A 25 million. (N) B 2.5 million. (Y) C More than 25 million. (R)

4 Madison's mom works at ...

A a building company on Paces Ferry Road. (C) B the CNN studios. (N) C Atlanta airport. (P)

5 Who is Dan?

A Madison's dad. (Y) B B Madison's teacher. (M) C Mrs Young's boss. (E)

6 Why didn't Madison go to her mom's workplace on TYCTWD?

A Because there was an explosion at CNN studios. (S) B Because they were in a traffic jam. (D)

C Because her mom thought it might be dangerous at the airport. (O)

7 The idea behind the TYCTWD is ...

A to introduce kids to the world of work. (K) B to give teachers a free day. (P)

C to interest students in the company they visit. (Y)

b) Write the letters next to your answers in a) in the correct order to find the missing word:

CNN is a worldwide 24-hour TV news ____________ which was founded in Atlanta.

8 WORDS Opposites ▸ p. 79

a) Find and write pairs of opposites.

cloudy • excellent • smart • soft • dead
fantastic • minority • fat
advantage • better • pick up • weak

hard • disadvantage • failure • alive
drop off • strong • skinny • stupid
cloudless • majority • worse • awful

cloudy	–	cloudless	____ – ____			____ – ____	
____	–	____	____ – ____			____ – ____	
____	–	____	____ – ____			____ – ____	
____	–	____	____ – ____			____ – ____	

5108

b) Write five sentences in your exercise book. Use a pair of opposites from a) in each sentence.

My brother thinks game shows are fantastic, but my dad thinks they're awful.

9 READING COURSE Part 4: Summer jobs in the US (Drawing conclusions)

► p. 79 • SF (p. 151)

a) Read the magazine article carefully and underline the main facts.

When summer comes, for most teens it means lots of free time, in the US usually from May to August. Some students go to summer camps or go on vacation with family. The ones who stay at home often take part in organized sports programmes or just hang out with friends. But many teens need money, for their families and for themselves, so they try to organize a job for the summer vacation. (1)

What kind of summer vacation jobs do teens do? Younger teens look for jobs in their home towns. About 25% have jobs in restaurants, about 25% help out in shops, 11% have an office job[1]. The rest do garden work or work for a pizza service. Some work at petrol stations and wash cars. (2)

We looked at statistics and found that now there are not as many summer jobs for teen workers as in past years. Why is this? We spoke to high school students in three US states. Here are some of their comments: Matt B., 16, from Germantown, Tennessee, said: 'I have a part-time job in a supermarket during the school year and I'm looking for a summer job too. I want to work because I need the money for college[2] later. The problem is that there aren't many jobs for teens. Adults who have lost their jobs and seniors[3] who need money are also looking for low-paid[4] work, so they get the jobs.' (3)

15-year-old Carol S. from San José, California said: 'There are lots of summer jobs here because of all the tourists. My sister is 18. She has work experience and she's at university, so she can work for longer than 3 months in summer. She has no problem getting a job, but it's more difficult for me.' (4)

'A lot of kids in my grade apply for[5] a summer workplace, but mostly without success. Kids our age only get boring jobs and not much money. Some employers[6] think that older people work harder and better. Some have the opinion that teenagers want money but don't really want to work for it. But we have to start somewhere. We need early work experience,' said 15-year-old Guy C. from Missouri City, Texas, 'but sometimes it's hard to get.' (5)

b) In which paragraphs does the text give direct information about the following? Write the paragraph number.

- how much summer vacation high school students have: paragraph ____
- how high school students spend the summer vacation: paragraph ____
- what kind of work high school students do: paragraph ____

c) The text says that now there are not as many summer jobs for high school students as in the past. Why is this? Find facts in the text which explain the reasons, and write the line number(s). Then draw a conclusion about the reasons.

Jobs that high school students could do are given to adults without work and to seniors who

d) **Extra** *Imagine you were a high school student in the States. Why would you like to work in the summer vacation? What kind of job would you like to do?*

I would try to get a summer vacation job because three months is a long time. I think it can be very boring if you do nothing. I always need money too. I think I would like to work in an ice cream place or ...

[1] office job ['ɒfɪs] *Büroarbeit* [2] college ['kɒlɪdʒ] [3] senior ['siːniə(r)] *Senior/in* [4] low-paid [ləʊ] *schlecht bezahlt* [5] apply for [ə'plaɪ] *sich bewerben* [6] employer [ɪm'plɔɪə(r)] *Arbeitgeber/in*

10 WORDS It wasn't washable! (Word building *-able*) ▸ p. 79

a) Match the adjectives with their meanings.

1 washable	• good enough to eat
2 eatable	• you can enjoy it
3 enjoyable	• you can wash it without problems
4 usable	• too difficult to pronounce[1]
5 unthinkable	• good enough to use
6 readable	• easy or interesting to read
7 unpronounceable	• impossible to imagine, too bad to think about

b) Now choose adjectives from a) to complete the sentences.

1 My MP3 player is old but it's still usable ________.

2 We had a great time in Atlanta. It was a very ____________ holiday.

3 I have an English friend who's learning German.

He thinks some German words are ____________.

4 I think I've lost my cellphone. That would be ____________!

5310 5 That hamburger is still in the fridge. Yuck! I don't think it's ____________ any more.

11 I've known her for four years (Present perfect with 'for') ▸ p. 79 • GF 6a (p. 168)

Answer the questions. Use the present perfect and ***for****.*

1 Is Madison your friend? – Yes/know/four years

Yes, she is. I have known her for four years.

2 Has Madison got a new computer? – Yes/have/two weeks

Yes, she has. She ____________

3 Does Madison's mom work for CNN?
– Yes/work there/three years

____

____

4 Is Madison in a school sports team?
– Yes/be/in basketball team/six months

____

____

5 Does Madison want to take part in TYCTWD?
– Yes/want to visit her mom's workplace/a year

____

[1] pronounce [prə'naʊns]

12 How long has she worked for CNN? (Present perfect with *'for'*) ▸ *p. 79 • GF 6a (p. 168)*

Ask questions with 'How long ...' about the statements. Then write answers with the information in brackets and ***for****.*

1 Madison's mom works for CNN. (about three years)

How long has she worked for CNN? – She has worked there for about three years.

2 Madison is at Martin Luther King High School. (one year)

____

3 Madison and her mom are in the traffic jam. (20 minutes)

____

4 The traffic downtown is bad. (two months)

5412 ____________________

Info box

Atlanta is ...
- one of the cleanest cities in the USA.
- maybe the 'greenest' city in the USA because of the green oak trees[1] that line[2] its streets.

Atlanta has ...
- the world's busiest international airport with over 77 million passengers[3] a year.
- 32 streets with the name 'Peachtree'.
- 54 parks.
- 41 golf courses.

13 Blue box: German 'seit' (since/for) ▸ *p. 80, p. 191*

A reporter for a local TV station is asking tourists some questions about their stay in Atlanta. Her first question is: 'How long have you been in Atlanta?' Complete what the tourists say with ***since*** *or* ***for****.*

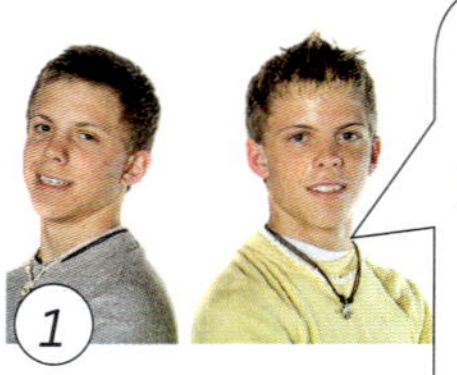

1 We've been here *since* yesterday. We love it.

2 I've been here ______ a week now. It's a great city.

3 ______ my birthday last week.

4 ______ last Sunday. I'm visiting friends.

5 ______ about five days now.

6 I've been here ______ ten years – I live here!

5413

[1] oak tree [əʊk] *Eiche* [2] line [laɪn] *säumen* [3] passenger ['pæsɪndʒə(r)] *Passagier*

Now you

*In your exercise book, write a sentence each with **since** and **for**. How long have you …*

1 lived in your village, town or city?
2 been in your school class?
3 known your English teacher?
4 had your pet, MP3 player or computer?

I've/We've lived in our town for about six years.
Or: *I've/We've lived in our town since 2004.*

14 LISTENING Malcolm X

▸ p. 81 • SF (p. 148) Track 12

Listen to the information about Malcolm X. Then complete the text.

Malcolm X was born in *Nebraska* in the year __________ . His real name was Malcolm __________ .

Like Martin Luther King he first became a ______________ , then a black speaker and civil rights leader.

But he ______________________ with King that non-violent protest was the only way. Black people

wanted ____________ , and many thought that it was coming too slowly. Malcolm X believed that blacks

should fight for equal[1] _____________ not with words, but with violent _________________ .

He said that white racists[2] only spoke the language of _______________ , not the language of peace[3].

Many young blacks followed him. There were riots[4] in the big cities of America and many people were

killed. Malcolm X was shot in 1965, while he was giving a ______________ in _________________ .

15 WORDS People and jobs

▸ p. 81

***a)** What's the word for somebody who …*

1 puts out fires? *firefighter*

2 goes to live and work in another country? ____________________

3 doesn't eat meat? ____________________

4 is the most important person in a US state government? ____________________

5 watches TV? ____________________

6 looks after your teeth? ____________________

7 is the leader of a town government? ____________________

5515 8 shows tourists round famous cities and sights? ____________________

***b)** Think of at least eight more jobs and write a list:*

____

____

[1] equal ['i:kwəl] *gleich* [2] racist ['reɪsɪst] *Rassist/in* [3] peace [pi:s] *Frieden*
[4] riot ['raɪət] *Ausschreitung, Aufruhr*

16 STUDY SKILLS Research ▸ p. 81 • SF (p. 146)

*a) What is important when you do research? Write **Y** (Yes) or **N** (No) next to the statements.*

1 use only Wikipedia N

2 use only one good source ____

3 use more than one source ____

4 try to use at least one English source ____

5 take notes in your own words ____

6 always take notes in your own language ____

7 always use complete sentences for your notes ____

8 look for answers to the 5 Ws (Who? What? When? Where? Why? + How?) ____

9 copy whole sentences from your sources ____

10 use only key words for internet search engines ____

*b) Now do research about **Muhammad Ali** (Cassius Clay), a famous African American, and what he did for black rights in the Civil Rights Movement. Write a short text with the most important information in your exercise book. Find answers to the following questions:*

- Who was Muhammad Ali?
- Why was his name known worldwide?
- Why was he in prison[1]?

17 WORDS Word building ▸ p. 81

a) Add a syllable from the box to make a new word.

-able (2x) • ~~dis-~~ • -er (2x) • -ful • il- • im- • -less (2x) • non- • un-

1 dis agree	4 support ____	7 end ____	10 success ____
2 break ____	5 ____ possible	8 ____ violent	11 ____ legal
3 wait ____	6 home ____	9 ____ healthy	12 do ____

b) Choose five words from a) and write a sentence with each.

1 My friend thinks growing up in two cultures makes life difficult, but I disagree.

2 ____

3 ____

4 ____

5 ____

5617 6 ____

[1] prison ['prɪzn] *Gefängnis*

18 Extra Background File
TOWARDS THE AFRICAN-AMERICAN DREAM

▸ pp. 82–83

a) *Read pp. 82–83 of your student's book again and complete the information below.*

1 In 2006 12.4% of the US population were black.

2 In 2004 ______ of the black population were without jobs.

3 The average black family had about $ ______ less to spend per year than the average white family.

4 Statistics say that in 2003 there were about ______ times more poor black people than poor white people.

5 In 2005 ______ of black students left school without a high school diploma.

6 In 2005 ______ of NBA players were black.

7 In the sport ______, 65% of the players are black.

8 In the three sports ______, ______ and ______, very few players are black.

9 In 2009 Barack Obama became the first African-American ______.

b) *Write about African-American musicians in a few sentences. Use your own words.*

c) *Answer the questions about the Rodney King riots.*

1 Where and when did the Rodney King riots take place?

2 Who was Rodney King and what happened to him?

3 How do we know what exactly happened to Rodney King?

4 What happened to the policemen? ______

5 Why were there terrible riots in Los Angeles?

d) *From what you have read, do you think that today black Americans have the same chances as white Americans? Think of the areas education and jobs, politics, sports, music. Write a paragraph in your exercise book.* I think that black Americans ...

19 WORKING WITH THE TEXT Melba's story ▸ pp. 89–92

a) Read p. 89 of your student's book again. Are the statements right or wrong? Write R or W.

1 After slavery ended, black people were segregated from white people for about a hundred years. R

2 There were separate schools for white children and for black children. ______

3 Only schools were segregated. ______

4 Schools for black children were just as good as schools for white children. ______

5 All states wanted to keep the new law against segregation in schools. ______

b) Now read the story about Melba on pp. 90–91 again. What did these people do? Write one sentence each.

1 The ticket man didn't let Melba ride on the merry-go-round and called her 'nigger'.

2 The Supreme Court ______

3 A teacher at Melba's all-black school ______

4 Most of the white students at Central High School ______

5 A white Californian family ______

c) Go through the text and write notes about the brave things Melba did.

NOTES

______

d) Do you think Melba was a hero[1]? Use your notes from c) and write a short essay (100–120 words) in your exercise book.

Black student tries to get through the National Guard line.

Central High School, Little Rock, Arkansas

[1] hero ['hɪərəʊ] *Held/in*

1 Write the missing words.

1 Madison's mom works for the TV news ______________ CNN.

2 Madison's favourite programmes are weekly crime and drama ______________ .

3 When Madison knew the date of Martin Luther King's death, her dad was ______________ .

4 Madison was really ______________ that she couldn't go to the airport with her mom.

5 Shirley Franklin was elected first African-American woman ______________ of Atlanta in 2002.

5901 6 Martin Luther King, leader of the US ______________ Movement, came from Atlanta.

2 Since or for?

Madison has been at her friend's ...

1 __________ 4 o'clock. 2 __________ at least three hours.

5902 3 __________ a long time. 4 __________ this morning.

3 Ask questions with How long ...? + present perfect.

1 Madison is at the MLK Center. How long ______________ there?

2 The Youngs have a new flat screen TV. How long ______________ it?

5903 3 Madison and her parents live in Atlanta. How long ______________ there?

4 During or while?

1 The phone rang three times ______________ Madison was watching her favourite programme.

5904 2 The phone rang three times ______________ Madison's favourite programme.

5 STUDY SKILLS Research

Find and tick (✓) the five correct sentences.

When you look for information on the internet or in books, ...

- use only one good source. ____
- use at least one English source. ____
- take notes in full sentences. ____
- use your own words. ____ (5905)
- use more than one source. ____
- think of the 5 Ws. ____
- say what your sources are. ____

20 points

Now you

5906 5907 *How much TV do you watch every day? When do you watch? What kind of programmes do you watch and why? Write about television and you (about 100 words). Use your exercise book.*

Jetzt kann ich ...	Sehr gut!	OK	Verbessern!
HÖREN: Ich kann ...			
... längere Texte und Geschichten verstehen, auch wenn ich einige Wörter nicht kenne.	☐	☐	☐
... aus Listenings (z.B. öffentliche Durchsagen) Details richtig heraushören.	☐	☐	☐
... den Akzent britischer und amerikanischer Sprecher/innen heraushören.	☐	☐	☐
SPRECHEN: Ich kann ...			
... anhand von Bildern eine Stadt und ihre Umgebung beschreiben.	☐	☐	☐
... meine Meinung zu Themen im Unterricht (z.B. gesunde Lebensmittel und Essgewohnheiten, Unterschiede zwischen amerikanischen und deutschen Schulen) frei äußern, auch wenn ich Fehler mache.	☐	☐	☐
... über Filme und Fernsehsendungen sprechen.	☐	☐	☐
LESEN: Ich ...			
... weiß, wie man die Hauptaussage (*main idea*), die Beispiele (*examples*) und Begründungen (*reasons*) in einem Sachtext erkennen kann.	☐	☐	☐
... kann in einem Sachtext Schlussfolgerungen aus gesammelten Fakten ziehen, wobei sich die Fakten an verschiedenen Stellen im Text befinden können.	☐	☐	☐
... kann eine *timeline* geschichtlicher Ereignisse richtig verstehen.	☐	☐	☐
SCHREIBEN: Ich kann ...			
... eine Zusammenfassung (*Summary*) eines Textes schreiben, indem ich die Hauptereignisse und das Wichtigste zu den 5 Ws mit eigenen Worten wiedergebe. Detaillierte Beschreibungen und direkte Rede lasse ich dabei weg.	☐	☐	☐
... eine Geschichte zu Ende schreiben.	☐	☐	☐
... eine E-mail über einen Film oder eine Fernsehsendung schreiben.	☐	☐	☐
... einen Brief mit der Bitte um Informationen verfassen.	☐	☐	☐
LAND UND LEUTE: Ich ...			
... weiß einiges über das Leben an einer amerikanischen High School (z.B. das Notensystem A–F).	☐	☐	☐
... weiß, was *extracurriculars* sind und dass sie an amerikanischen High Schools sehr wichtig sind.	☐	☐	☐
... habe einiges über Hermann, Missouri, gelernt (z.B. Bevölkerung, Größe, Landschaft, Industrie, Geschichte).	☐	☐	☐
... weiß, dass in Hermann deutsche Traditionen z.B. (Volksfeste) gepflegt werden.	☐	☐	☐
... habe viel über die Stadt Atlanta und ihre Geschichte gelernt.	☐	☐	☐
... habe einiges über Martin Luther King und die Geschichte der *Civil Rights Movement* gelernt.	☐	☐	☐

Jetzt kann ich ...	Sehr gut!	OK	Verbessern!
GRAMMATIKVERSTÄNDNIS: Ich kann ...			
... einige Nomen, die im Englischen keine Pluralform haben, richtig verwenden (z.B. *homework/information/news is ...*). Mit solchen nicht zählbaren Nomen verwende ich die Mengenangaben *some/any, a lot of/(not) much.*			
... den bestimmten Artikel richtig einsetzen. Wenn ein Nomen für einen abstrakten Begriff (z.B. *life, history, health*) oder eine Stoffbezeichnung (z.B. *air, oil*) ganz allgemein gebraucht wird, steht es ohne *the*. *The* verwende ich bei solchen Nomen, wenn sie näher bestimmt werden (z.B. *Life is exciting for Timo. / The life of Missouri farmers is interesting.*).			
... das *past perfect* für Handlungen und Zustände in der Vorvergangenheit richtig bilden und anwenden (z.B. *I didn't buy the CD because I had left my money at home.*).			
... das *present perfect* mit *since* und *for* verstehen und richtig anwenden. Damit drücke ich einen Zustand aus, der in der Vergangenheit begonnen hat und jetzt noch andauert. Mit *since* gebe ich einen Zeitpunkt an. Mit *for* gebe ich einen Zeitraum an (z.B. *I've known Kim since 2005/ for five years.*).			
VOKABELVERSTÄNDNIS: Ich kann ...			
... AE-Wörter für die Schule (z.B. *elementary school, middle school, schedule, grades, extracurriculars*) richtig verwenden.			
... Wörter für Lebensmittel (z.B. *muesli, beans, poultry, whole-grain products*) richtig verwenden.			
... Medien-Wörter, insbesondere für das Fernsehen (z.B. *prime time, crime series, rerun, documentary, channels*) richtig verwenden.			
... Adjektive mit der Endung *-able* richtig bilden (z.B. *breakable, doable*).			
SKILLS – LERNEN UND ARBEITEN: Ich ...			
... weiß, dass man beim Recherchieren (*research*) mehrere Quellen benutzt und Notizen mit eigenen Worten schreibt.			
... weiß, wie ich das Internet zur Recherche mithilfe von gut gewählten *key words* erfolgreich nutzen kann.			

WAS ICH FÜR MEIN ENGLISCHLERNEN GETAN HABE: Ich habe ...	häufig	manchmal	nie
... die Angaben im Grammar File in meinem Buch aufmerksam gelesen.			
... versucht, die Lern- und Arbeitstechniken im Skills File in meinem Buch im Unterricht und bei den Hausaufgaben anzuwenden.			
... bereits gelernte Vokabeln und Grammatik häufig aufgefrischt.			

WIE ICH MICH VERBESSERN KÖNNTE: Ich könnte ...

- ... im Unterricht aktiver mitarbeiten. ☐
- ... häufiger ein zweisprachiges Wörterbuch benutzen. ☐
- ... englische Websites zu Unterrichtsthemen gezielt recherchieren. ☐
- ... mir englische Notizen von englischsprachigen Websites machen. ☐
- ... mir häufiger Texte von meiner CD anhören. ☐

1 WORDS Lists ▸ *after Unit 1*

Find and write the group words or phrases at the top of the lists. Then write the words in the correct lists.

transport · championship · *tube* · sport · people · ambulance · editor · holidays · sights · paramedic · ferry · suitcase · ski slope · tram · sunglasses · plane · running track · neighbour · tent · helicopter · goalkeeper · adult · stadium · husband · athletics · presenter · sea · beach

1 T*ransport*	2 S______	3 P______	4 H______
tube			

6201

2 Questions (Simple present: questions) ▸ *after Unit 1*

Make questions with question words. Ask about the people in brackets and use the simple present.

1 Caitlin lives in New York. (Madison?) *Where does Madison live?*

2 Madison comes from Atlanta. (Jake?) ______

3 Caitlin likes cycling and hiking. (Madison and Luis?) ______

4 Luis speaks two languages. (Jake?) ______

6202 5 Jakes starts school at 8.20. (Luis and Caitlin?) ______

3 Get it right! Spelling: *-ing*-forms ▸ *after Unit 1*

Write the -ing-forms of the verbs in the correct lists.

call · *change* · *get* · hurry · joke · lose · run · stop · swim · take · try · use · walk · wear · win

+ ing	~~e~~ + ing	(2x)+ ing
calling	*changing*	*getting*

4 The taxi is waiting (Simple present or present progressive) ▸ after Unit 1

Complete with the correct form of the verb in brackets: simple present or present progressive.

Mum Come on! Hurry! The taxi *is waiting* (wait). We *have to* (have to) leave for the airport now.

Sam I ______ (still, pack) my bag. The plane ______ (not leave) until lunchtime. Why ______ (Mum, always, get) nervous every time somebody ______ (go) on holiday?

Ann Somebody ______ (always, forget) something. Oh. But Dad ______ (not get) nervous, does he? What ______ (he, do) just now?

Sam He ______ (already, sit) in the taxi, I ______ (think).

6304 *Dad* Well, no, I ______ (not sit) in the taxi. Erm ... I ______ (look) for my passport[1] ...

5 When did you go? (Simple past: questions) ▸ after Unit 1

Make B's questions. Use the words in brackets and the simple past.

	A	B
1	I went to the USA in June. (When?)	*When did you go?*
2	I stayed in San Francisco. (Where?)	______
3	I stayed there for three weeks. (How long?)	______
4	I saw lots of famous sights. (What?)	______

6305

6 We went up the Stratosphere Tower (Simple past) ▸ after Unit 1

Complete the dialogue with simple past forms of the verbs in brackets.

Kate Tom! You're back! How *was* (be) your trip to Las Vegas? *Did you have* (you, have) a good time?

Where ______ (you, go) and what ______ (you, see)?

Tom Well, I ______ (do) a tour of all the theme hotels with my cousin Eli, and my aunt and uncle ______ (plan) a day tour to Death Valley for me. One evening we ______ (go) up the Stratosphere Tower. I ______ (not enjoy) going up in the fast lift much. I just ______ (close) my eyes and ______ (try) to think of something else. But I ______ (take) some cool photos from the top.

We ______ (not go) to any shows – too expensive.

6306 And no, before you ask, I ______ (not meet) my dream girl ...

[1] passport ['pɑːspɔːt] *Reisepass*

7 It was raining (Simple past or past progressive) ▸ *after Unit 1*

Underline the correct verb form in the brackets.

1 When we (were arriving/arrived) in New York, it (rained/was raining).

2 The sun suddenly (came/was coming) out when we (were taking/took) photos of the Statue of Liberty.

3 We (saw/were seeing) lots of interesting people when we (were walking/walked) through Central Park.

4 Just as I (was crossing/crossed) Times Square, a man (was asking/asked) me something in German.

5 Yesterday we (cycled/were cycling) onto Brooklyn Bridge and (watched/were watching) the boats below.

6407

6 As I (was shopping/shopped) in Macy's, I suddenly (found/was finding) out that I had forgotten my money.

8 WORDS People or things? ▸ *after Unit 1*

Write the words in two groups.

adult • *cooker* • collector • counter • driver • editor • elevator • eraser • firefighter • guy • hijacker • immigrant • laughter • leader • leather • mirror • painter • pepper • quarter • sailor • skyscraper • sleepover • supporter • waiter • writer

People: *adult,* ____________________

____

Things: *cooker,* ____________________

____

9 Verbs: irregular verb forms ▸ *after Unit 1*

Complete the lists with verb forms.

become	*became*	become	______	______	forgotten
______	______	chosen	hold	______	______
come	______	______	ring	______	______
______	drank	______	______	______	stood
fall	______	______	______	______	taught
______	______	felt	______	wore	______
fly	______	______	______	______	written

10 They've all been there (Simple past or present perfect) ▸ after Unit 1

Complete with the simple past or the present perfect.

Lucy, Brad and Kelly _have all been_ (all, be) to the Grand Canyon.

They _went_ (go) there in the last summer vacation.

Here's what they ________ (say) after their trip.

Kelly The Grand Canyon is the most exciting thing I ________ (ever, see). And walking on the glass floor is the scariest thing I ________ (ever, do) in my life.

Lucy We ________ (stay) at the Canyon for three days. I ________ (never, see) anything so beautiful. It ________ (be) so awesome!

Brad We ________ (enjoy) every minute of the trip. I ________ (visit) some cool places in the US, but nothing like the Grand Canyon.

6510

11 If I have enough money, ... (Conditional sentences 1 and 2) ▸ after Unit 1

Complete the sentences with the correct form of the verb.

1 A: If I _have_ (have) enough money in summer, maybe I _'ll go_ (go) to the USA with a friend.

2 B: Great! Where ________ (you, stay) if you go?

3 A: Well, maybe California, for three weeks. We'd take our camping gear if we ________ (stay) at places along the coast.

4 B: Cool. You ________ (be able to) swim in the Pacific every day if you were close to a beach.

If I ever ________ (visit) California, I'd want to see the theme parks[1], Disneyland or SeaWorld.

6512

5 A: That would be cool too. But if we went to theme parks, we ________ (spend) all our money in the first week!

[1] theme park ['θiːm] *Themenpark* (*Freizeitpark*)

12 Greg's presentation *(have to, be allowed to, be able to)* ▸ *after Unit 1*

Complete with the correct form and tense of the verb in brackets: simple present, simple past or will-future

I *have to* (have to) give a presentation about George Washington, but my computer is broken. Dad is in London and I ________ (not be allowed to) use his computer when he isn't at home. Yesterday I ________ (have to) go to the library. I ________ (be able to) get some information, but not enough. I ________ (have to) ask my friend for help tomorrow. I hope he ________ (be able to) download some stuff for me. If I don't finish my presentation, I ________ (not be allowed to) go to the disco next Saturday.

13 WORDS Word families (Nouns from verbs) ▸ *after Unit 1*

Write a noun from each verb. Sometimes the noun is the same as the verb. If you know two nouns, write both.

Verb	Noun	Verb	Noun
1 announce	– *announcement*	9 explain	– ________
2 argue	– ________	10 fly	– ________
3 arrive	– ________	11 hope	– ________
4 begin	– ________	12 invite	– ________
5 collect	– ________	13 joke	– ________
6 cook	– ________	14 live	– ________
7 copy	– ________	15 mix	– ________
8 draw	– ________	16 report	– ________

14 Ride carefully! (Adjective or adverb) ▸ *after Unit 1*

Complete with the adjective or adverb form of the word in brackets.

1 My dad is a taxi-driver in New York, so he knows the city traffic *well* (good).

2 He always tells me to ride ________ (careful) when I'm on my bike.

3 He says most people drive ________ (safe), but there are always some ________ (bad) drivers who go too ________ (fast).

4 You have to be ________ (careful) on the sidewalks too. Some kids skate ________ (dangerous), so you're not ________ (safe) anywhere in a big city, says my dad. He worries too much.

6615

15 USA: People and places (who or that) ▸ after Unit 1

*Complete the sentences with **who** or **that**.*

1 New York and San Francisco are the cities ________ European tourists want to visit most.

2 Michael Phelps is the swimmer ________ won 8 gold medals for the USA in the 2008 Olympic Games.

3 Beach volleyball is a sport ________ first came from California. It's now an Olympic team sport.

4 Frédéric-Auguste Bartholdi was born in France in 1834. He is the man ________ designed the Statue of Liberty.

6716 5 Theodore (Teddy) Roosevelt was the US President ________ gave the teddy bear its name in 1902.

16 The Grand Canyon (Contact clauses) ▸ after Unit 1

***a)** Find six sentences where you don't need **who** or **that**. Write them again as contact clauses (without **who** or **that**). You need the letters in brackets in b).*

US park rangers protect the animals that live in the national parks (I) and the tourists who visit every year (N). There is lots of information that the rangers can give you (A). For example, they can tell you about the Native Americans who first lived in the Canyon area (N). In national parks there are lots of things that tourists must or mustn't do (E). There are rules[1] that you must follow if you want to be safe (A). One rule says you mustn't make fires in places that could be dangerous (D).
There are lots of things that you can do at the Grand Canyon National Park (D). There is a free bus that you can take along the rim (N). If you want to hike, there are trails that are easy and safe (A). There are also trails that tourists mustn't take if they aren't fit (V).

1 *There is lots of information the rangers can give you.* ____ *A*

2 ________________________ ____

3 ________________________ ____

4 ________________________ ____

5 ________________________ ____

6 ________________________ ____

***b)** Write down the letters in brackets after the six sentences. Then put them in the right order to find the name of a US state.*

6717 The state is ▶ ________________.

[1] rule [ruːl] *Regel*

17 On holiday at the Grand Canyon (Word order) ▸ *after Unit 1*

Complete the sentences with the words in brackets in the correct order.

1 Caitlin and her family (every year/to a national park/go).

Caitlin and her family go to a national park every year.

2 Luis and his friends raised money before (on the trip/they/went).

______

3 The youth group stayed (for three days/at the canyon).

______

4 All the kids were excited because (so amazing/is/the Grand Canyon).

______

5 Luis and his friends had lots of fun when (their own meals/cooked/they).

______

6 Jake was happy because (a condor/saw/he).

______

18 WORDS Odd one out ▸ *after Unit 1*

a) Find and write the odd one out. Then count and write the letters.

1 trousers	• shorts	• jeans	• clothes	*clothes*	(3)	*o*
2 pepper	• ruler	• supporter	• elevator	______	(5)	______
3 cow	• turkey	• bacon	• pig	______	(2)	______
4 California	• Missouri	• Ontario	• Georgia	______	(4)	______
5 ranger	• cooker	• firefighter	• caretaker	______	(4)	______
6 went	• saw	• swum	• wrote	______	(4)	______
7 drum	• flute	• trumpet	• ceilidh	______	(7)	______
8 cathedral	• synagogue	• mosque	• hostel	______	(6)	______

b) Put the letters in the right order and find the word that completes the sentence:

▶ On their way to the Grand Canyon, Jake and his dad drove through *O* ______.

19 Find the mistakes

► after Unit 1 • SF (p. 155)

Find and correct the mistakes in Heike's postcard to her cousin in the US.

Hello Rachel,

We stay here in Hamburg for one week. Just now we sit in a café, so I write postcards. Yesterday we have taken a boat trip round the harbour and in the evening we have seen a musical. It's nice here. If you would come to visit Germany, you'd like it here too, I think. Maybe tomorrow we go to the famous Hamburg Michel. It's a church with a big clock tower, who all the tourists climb. Mum want to go to a museum – but I don't enjoy to look round museums!

Love, Heike

are staying, __________

20 WORDS Word fields

► after Unit 1

How many words can you add to the word fields? Look at the pictures for help and use the Dictionary in your student's book (pp. 194–224).

In a national park

Downtown

1 In a national park: *river, hiking trail,* __________

2 Downtown: *shopping centre,* __________

- Hier kannst du deine Antworten im Checkpoint überprüfen. Falls du Probleme mit den jeweiligen Aufgaben hattest, folge den Lernhilfen in der rechten Spalte. Die Verweise beziehen sich auf dein Schülerbuch oder dein Workbook.
- Deine Punktzahl kannst du ermitteln, indem du dir für jede richtige Lösung einen Punkt gibst. Schreib deine Gesamtpunktzahl in das gelbe Kästchen unten links.

1 What are these places?

1 deli
2 downtown
3 skyscraper(s)
4 block
5 apartment
6 gas station

6 P.

- Lies dir im Skills File in deinem Buch (S. 143) den Abschnitt zu *Learning words* durch.
- Lern die Wörter mithilfe des Vocabulary (Buch: S. 174–179).

2 Write the missing words.

1 ground floor – first floor
2 timetable – schedule
3 (school) year – grade
4 rucksack – backpack
5 rubbish – garbage
6 chips – French fries

6 P.

- Lern die unterschiedlichen BE- und AE-Wörter mithilfe der blauen Kästen auf den S. 175, 176 und 178 in deinem Buch.

3 If or when?

1 when 2 if 3 when

3 P.

- Wiederhole die Übung 11 im Practice-Teil (Buch: S. 24).

4 Complete the sentences with gerunds.

1 planning
2 meeting
3 finding
4 taking
5 travelling

5 P.

- Schau dir Grammar File 1 zum Gerundium in deinem Buch (S. 161–162) oder hinten im Grammar File *kompakt* in deinem Workbook (S. 76–77) noch einmal an.
- Löse die Aufgaben 4 (S. 21), 6 und 7 (S. 22) im Practice-Teil deines Buchs.

Now you (Ideas)

Good things: a rich, multi-cultural city with world-famous sights/important tourist centre/interesting history (Ellis Island, Liberty, etc)/ a lot to see (Broadway theatres, concerts, opera, famous museums, art galleries)/Central Park/ international airports/subway/a city that never sleeps is exciting

Bad things: traffic day and night/noise/crowded city streets, often dirty/can take a long time to get around/poor areas (e. g. the Bronx)/expensive city to live in, high prices for houses and apartments

- Um Ideen über New York zu sammeln, kannst du dir die Unit 1 in deinem Buch noch einmal anschauen oder im Internet recherchieren.
- Lies dir im Skills File den Abschnitt zu *Brainstorming* durch (Buch: S. 153), um deine Ideen besser ordnen zu können.
- Um das *simple present* sicherer zu beherrschen, kannst du im Revision-Block in deinem Workbook die Übungen 2 (S. 62) und 4 (S. 63) machen.
- Trage deinen kurzen Vortrag über New York laut vor.

Ich habe ______ Punkte von 20.

20–18	Sehr gut. Weiter so!
17–15	Schon recht gut.
Unter 15	Genauer lernen!

Falls du Probleme hattest:

1 Write the missing words.

5 P.

1 *grapes*
2 *minority*
3 *illegal*
4 *discriminate*
5 *population*

- Guck dir im Skills File in deinem Buch den Abschnitt zu *Learning words* an (S. 143).
- Lern die Wörter (Buch: S. 180–184).

2 Complete the sentences with passive forms.

4 P.

1 *are grown*
2 *was* first *found*
3 *is produced*
4 *were killed*

- Lies dir Grammar File 2a–c zum Passiv noch einmal durch (Buch: S. 163, Workbook: S. 77).
- Löse die Aufgaben 5 und 6 im Practice-Teil (Buch: S. 44).

3 Complete the word families.

6 P.

1 *experience*
2 *production/product*
3 *industrial*
4 *succeed*
5 *discrimination*
6 *be prejudiced*

- Schau dir die Wörter noch einmal im Vocabulary an und lern sie (Buch: S. 180–181).
- Im Revision-Block gibt es auch eine Übung zu *word families* (Workbook: S. 66, Übung 13).

4 Complete with skim or scan.

3 P.

1 *skim* 2 *scan* 3 *skim*

- Im Skills File kannst du dir die wichtigen Punkte zu *skimming* und *scanning* noch einmal anschauen (Buch: S. 150, Workbook: S. 74).
- Mach die Übung 4 im Practice-Teil noch einmal (Buch: S. 43).

Now you (Ideas)

For many people California is a dreamland because ... sunny weather all year/beautiful national parks/rich multi-cultural state
Industries: *farming (wine, fruit and vegetables)/Silicon Valley (computer and software industry)/movie industry/ theme parks*
Tourist activities: *enjoy beautiful beaches/drive along the coast/go surfing/visit national parks/visit theme parks/see cities like San Francisco and L.A. with many tourist attractions*
Problems of the state: *danger of earthquakes/forest fires almost every year/dirty air in big cities/homeless people/ illegal immigrants*

- Suche in der Unit 2 in deinem Buch nach Informationen über die relevanten Punkte zu Kalifornien. Du kannst auch im Internet recherchieren.
- Die *writing skills* kannst du dir im Skills File noch einmal anschauen (Buch: S. 154–155, Workbook: S. 75).
- Um sicherer bei Beschreibungen zu werden, kannst du im Revision-Block die Aufgaben 14–16 lösen (Workbook: S. 66–67).

Ich habe ______ Punkte von 18.

18–16	Sehr gut. Weiter so!
15–13	Schon recht gut.
Unter 13	Genauer lernen!

Falls du Probleme hattest:

1 Write the missing words.

1 countryside
2 health
3 contains
4 whole-grain
5 average

5 P.

- Lies dir im Skills File den Abschnitt zu *Learning words* durch (Buch: S. 143).
- Lern die Wörter mithilfe des Vocabulary (Buch: S. 184–188).

2 Add the where you need it.

1 Jake: the
Timo: –
2 – The

4 P.

- Wie du den bestimmten Artikel *the* gebrauchst, erfährst du im Grammar File 4 (Buch: S. 166, Workbook: S. 79).
- Löse die Aufgabe 10 im Practice-Teil (Buch: S. 66).

3 Put in a/an, some, much or many.

1 much some an
2 many some

5 P.

- Über die Besonderheiten von nicht zählbaren Nomen erfährst du etwas im Grammar File 3 (Buch: S. 165, Workbook: S. 78).
- Wiederhole die Übungen 7 und 8 im Practice-Teil (Buch: S. 64).

4 Find and tick (✓) the four correct statements.

- give only the most important information from the original text. ✓
- tell the reader what the text or story is about in the first few sentences. ✓
- explain **who** does **what**, **where**, **when** and **why**. ✓
- give lots of details. ___
- use the simple present and your own words. ✓
- use lots of adjectives for description and comparisons. ___

4 P.

- Im Skills File kannst du noch einmal nachlesen, was beim *summary writing* wichtig ist (Buch: S. 157).
- Schau dir auch den blauen Kasten auf S. 67 in deinem Buch an.

Now you (Ideas)

There are a few important differences between US and German schools. First, ... US school types: elementary, junior high, high school/school day is longer (afternoon school until 3 pm every day)/ hot lunch in school/US grade system (A–F)/ different classrooms for different subjects – students go to the classrooms/school bus for students is usual/ longer summer vacation, about 3 months/extracurricular activities and sports are important/ cheerleaders for school teams

- Informationen über amerikanische Schulen findest du in der Unit 3 in deinem Buch und in den Aufgaben 4–6 in deinem Workbook (S. 36–37).
- Ordne deine Gedanken und strukturiere deinen Text in sinnvolle Absätze (*Writing course*: Buch S. 154–155, Workbook S. 75).
- Um sicherer bei der Satzbildung zu werden, kannst du Übung 17 im Revision-Block machen (Workbook: S. 68).

Ich habe ______ Punkte von 18.

18–16	Sehr gut. Weiter so!
15–13	Schon recht gut.
Unter 13	Genauer lernen!

Falls du Probleme hattest:

1 Write the missing words.

1 network
2 series
3 impressed
4 disappointed
5 mayor
6 Civil Rights

6 P.

- Lern die Wörter (Buch: S. 189–193).

2 Since or for?

1 since
2 for
3 for
4 since

4 P.

- Im Grammar File 6 erfährst du, wie du *since* und *for* benutzt (Buch: S. 168, Workbook: S. 80).
- Schau dir auch den blauen Kasten zu 'seit' auf S. 191 in deinem Buch an.
- Löse die Aufgaben 9, 10 und 11a im Practice-Teil (Buch: S. 87–88).

3 Ask questions with How long …?

1 How long has she been there?
2 How long have they had it?
3 How long have they lived there?

3 P.

- Schau dir Grammar File 6 an (Buch: S. 168, Workbook: S. 80).
- Löse auch die Aufgaben 9 und 10 im Revision-Block, damit du das *present perfect* sicherer beherrscht (Workbook: S. 64–65).

4 During or while?

1 while
2 during

2 P.

- Im blauen Kasten auf S. 189 in deinem Buch kannst du nachlesen, wann du *during* und wann du *while* benutzen musst.

5 STUDY SKILLS Research

- use only one good source ______
- use more than one source ✓
- use at least one English source ✓
- think of the 5 Ws ✓
- take notes in full sentences ______
- say what your sources are ✓
- use your own words ✓

5 P.

- Im Skills File erfährst du, wie du beim Recherchieren am besten vorgehen solltest (Buch: S. 146).
- Lies dir auch den blauen Kasten zu *research* auf S. 81 in deinem Buch durch.

Now you (Ideas)

I'm (not) a TV fan/ I watch (don't watch) TV every day/ In my free time I like to do other things like sports or going out with friends/I could (couldn't) live without TV/ I watch TV for one to two hours a day/at the weekend/before I go to bed/after I have done my homework/ I only watch my favourite programmes/I like to watch the news/sports programmes/a soap opera/documentaries/quiz shows/I think … game shows/comedy shows/soap operas are good/bad/stupid/ interesting/funny, etc.

- Wichtige Wörter und Ideen zum Thema *TV* findest du in der Unit 4 in deinem Buch (S. 78).
- Strukturiere deinen Text (*Writing course*: Buch S. 154–155, Workbook S. 75).
- Um zu prüfen, wie gut du im Fehler finden und korrigieren bist, kannst du die Übung 19 im Revision-Block machen (Workbook: S. 69).

Ich habe ______ Punkte von 20.

20–18	Sehr gut. Weiter so!
17–15	Schon recht gut.
Unter 15	Genauer lernen!

LISTENING SKILLS

▶ *SF p. 148*

Vor dem Hören:

- Überlege, worum es in dem Hörtext gehen wird. Frag dich, was du schon über das Thema weißt.
- Lies die Aufgabe gut durch, damit du weißt, worauf du achten sollst:
  • auf die Hauptgedanken oder
  • auf bestimmte Informationen, wie z.B. Namen, Uhrzeit, Jahreszahlen.
- Bereite dich darauf vor, Notizen zu machen. Leg z.B. eine Tabelle oder Liste an.

Beim Hören:

- Achte auf Geräusche und unterschiedliche Stimmen. Was ein Sprecher/eine Sprecherin besonders betont, das ist wichtig!
- Wenn du gezielt nach Informationen suchst, denk an die Aufgabe und lass dich von anderen Einzelheiten nicht ablenken.
- Aufgepasst! Die Informationen, die du suchst, kommen vielleicht in einer anderen Reihenfolge vor, als du sie erwartest.
- Manche Signalwörter machen es dir leichter, den Hörtext zu verstehen:
  • Aufzählung: **and**, **another**, **too**
  • Gegensatz: **although**, **but**
  • Grund, Folge: **because**, **so**, **so that**
  • Vergleich: **larger/older/... than**, **more**, **most**
  • Reihenfolge: **before**, **after**, **then**, **next**, **later**, **when**, **at last**, **at the same time**

Nach dem Hören:

- Vervollständige deine Notizen sofort.
- Konzentriere dich beim zweiten Hören auf das, was du zuerst nicht gut verstanden hast.

READING COURSE – Zusammenfassung

▶ *SF pp. 150–151*

REVISION Working out the meaning of words
Was hilft dir, unbekannte Wörter zu verstehen?

1. **Bilder** zeigen oft die Dinge, die du im Text nicht verstehst. Wenn es Bilder zum Text gibt, dann schau sie dir vor dem Lesen genau an.
2. Oft hilft dir der **Textzusammenhang**, z.B. *When we **reached** the station, Judy went to the ticket machine to buy our tickets.*
3. Manche englischen Wörter werden **ähnlich wie im Deutschen** geschrieben oder ausgesprochen, z.B. **excellent**, **millionaire**, **nation**, **reality**.
4. Manchmal stecken in unbekannten Wörtern **bekannte Teile**, z.B. **friendliness**, **helpless**, **understandable**, **gardener**, **tea bag**, **waiting room**.

REVISION Skimming and Scanning

Beim **Skimming** überfliegst du einen Text schnell, um dir einen ersten **Überblick** zu verschaffen, worum es geht. Du willst herausfinden, ob ein Text, den du im Internet oder in einem Buch gefunden hast, überhaupt nützliche Informationen zu deinem Thema (z.B. für ein Referat) enthält. Achte beim Skimming auf:

- die **Überschrift**
- die **Zwischenüberschriften** und **hervorgehobene** Wörter oder Sätze
- die **Bilder** und **Bildunterschriften**
- den **ersten** und **letzten Satz** jedes Absatzes
- **Grafiken**, **Statistiken** und die **Quelle** des Textes

Beim **Scanning** suchst du in einem Text nach **bestimmten Informationen**, die z.B. für ein Referat wichtig sind. Dazu brauchst du nicht den gesamten Text zu lesen, sondern du suchst nach Schlüsselwörtern (**key words**) und liest nur dort genauer, wo du sie findest.

Finding the main ideas of a text

1. Jeder Text dreht sich um ein Thema oder hat eine Hauptaussage, z.B.
   Drinking soda is one of the worst things you can do to your health.
   Diese Hauptaussage findest du oft im **ersten Absatz**. Lies ihn deshalb besonders gründlich durch.
2. Die Hauptaussage wird in der Regel durch weitere Aussagen bzw. Gedanken unterstützt, z.B.
   Experts agree that sugary soft drinks and fast food are the main reasons why so many American teenagers are fat.
   Du findest sie oft im ersten oder letzten Satz der nachfolgenden Absätze.
3. Diese weiteren Aussagen bzw. Gedanken werden meist durch Beispiele und Begründungen ergänzt, z.B.
   About 7% of the calories that they take in come from soft drinks alone.

Drawing conclusions

1. Die einfachste Form des schlussfolgernden Lesens besteht darin, die Informationen aus verschiedenen Textstellen zusammenzuführen. Im Text auf S. 86 in deinem Buch z.B. musst du mehrere Textstellen anschauen, wenn du alle Gründe finden willst, warum Schüler/innen in den USA arbeiten gehen.
2. Manchmal steht die Antwort auf eine Frage nicht direkt im Text. Dann musst du sie dir erschließen. Im Text auf S. 86 geht es um die Frage, welche Auswirkungen das Arbeiten auf die schulischen Leistungen hat. Dafür musst du Fakten im Text finden, die etwas mit dieser Frage zu tun haben:

FACTS: students have an 11-hour work day; after work they're often too tired to do their homework = negative effects
working makes students more disciplined; they learn to organize their time = positive effects
CONCLUSION: for some students it's good, but for many it means bad grades

Tipp

Die folgenden Wörter oder Wendungen werden oft im Zusammenhang mit Begründungen oder Beispielen verwendet:
... % of ... are ... • **and so** • **because** • **e.g. / for example** • **etc.** • **for lots of reasons** • **this shows that** • **that's why**

MEDIATION SKILLS

▸ *SF p. 152*

Manchmal musst du zwischen zwei Sprachen vermitteln. Das nennt man mediation.
- Übersetze nicht alles wörtlich.
- Gib nur das Wesentliche weiter, lass Unwichtiges weg.
- Verwende kurze und einfache Sätze.
- Wenn du ein Wort nicht kennst, umschreibe es oder ersetze es durch ein anderes Wort.

REVISION Writing course – Zusammenfassung

▸ *SF pp. 154–155*

The steps of writing

1. Brainstorming – Ideen sammeln, dann sortieren (▸ *SF Brainstorming*).
2. Schreiben. Dabei achte darauf,
   - deine Sätze zu verbinden und auszubauen (*Writing better sentences*)
   - deinen Text gut zu strukturieren (*Using paragraphs*)
   - bei einem Bericht die 5 Ws abzudecken (*Writing a report*)
3. Deinen Text inhaltlich und sprachlich überprüfen (*Correcting your text*)

Writing better sentences

Eine Geschichte klingt interessanter, wenn du die Sätze mit **linking words** miteinander verbindest. Dabei gibt es mehrere Möglichkeiten:
- **Time phrases** wie **at 7 o'clock**, **every morning**, **a few minutes later**, **then**, **next** ...
- **Konjunktionen** wie **although**, **because**, **but**, **so** ... **that**, **that**, **when**, **while**
- **Relativpronomen** wie **that** und **who**
- Mit Adjektiven kannst du Personen, Orte oder Erlebnisse genauer und interessanter beschreiben. Vergleiche: **The man looked into the house.** ▸ **The young man looked into the empty house.**
- Mit Adverbien kannst du beschreiben, **wie** jemand etwas macht:
  The young man looked nervously into the empty house.

Using paragraphs

Ein längerer Text ist besser zu verstehen, wenn er in mehrere Absätze unterteilt ist:
- eine Einleitung (**beginning**)
  – hier schreibst du, worum es geht
- einen Hauptteil (**middle**)
  – hier schreibst du mehr über dein Thema
- einen Schluss (**end**)
  – hier bringst du den Text zu einem interessanten Ende.

Am Anfang eines Absatzes sind kurze, einleitende Sätze (**topic sentences**) gut, weil sie den Lesern sofort sagen, worum es geht, z. B.
1. Orte: **My trip to ... was fantastic. / ... is famous for ... / ... is a great place.**
2. Personen: **... is great/funny/interesting/clever ...**
3. Aktivitäten: **... is great fun. / Lots of people ... every day.**
- Beginne mit einem interessanten Einstiegssatz:
  You'll never guess what happened to me today! / Did I tell you that ...?
- Fang für jeden neuen Aspekt einen neuen Absatz an.
- Beende deinen Text mit einer Zusammenfassung oder etwas Persönlichem.

Writing a report – collecting and organizing ideas
- Gib dem Leser **eine schnelle Orientierung**, was passiert ist.
- Beginne mit **wichtigen Informationen** und gib erst dann Detailinformationen.
- Ein Bericht gibt immer Antworten auf die **5 Ws**:
  Who? What? When? Where? Why? und manchmal auch auf **How?**
- Verwende das **simple past**.

Correcting your text

Spelling mistakes

Lies deinen Text langsam, Wort für Wort, Buchstabe für Buchstabe. Wenn du unsicher bist, hilft dir ein Wörterbuch. Beachte folgende Regeln:

Tipp
- Manche Wörter haben Buchstaben, die man nicht spricht, aber schreibt, z. B. **knife**, **climb**.
- Manchmal ändert sich die Schreibweise, wenn ein Wort eine Endung erhält,
  z. B. **take** → **taking**, **terrible** → **terribly**, **lucky** → **luckily**, **try** → **tries** (**aber stay** → **stays**), **run** → **running**, **drop** → **dropped**.
- Beim Plural tritt manchmal noch ein **-e** zum **-s**, z. B. **church** → **churches**.

Grammar mistakes

Diese Tipps helfen dir, typische Fehler zu vermeiden:

Tipp
- Im **simple present** wird in der 3. Person Singular **-s** angehängt: **she knows**
- **Unregelmäßige Verben:** Manche Verben bilden die Formen des *simple past* und des Partizip Perfekt *(past participle)* unregelmäßig. Die unregelmäßigen Formen musst du lernen. Die Liste steht auf S. 258–259 in deinem Buch.
  go – went – gone; buy – bought – bought
- **Verneinung bei Vollverben:** Im *simple present* mit ***don't/ doesn't***, im *simple past* mit **didn't**, z. B. **He doesn't speak French, he didn't learn it at school.**
- **Satzstellung**: Im Englischen gilt immer (auch im Nebensatz):
  a) subject – verb – object (SVO)
  ... when I saw my brother. / ... als ich meinen Bruder sah.
  b) Orts- vor Zeitangabe **I bought a nice book in the city yesterday.**

Unit 1

GF 1 The gerund

▶ GF pp. 161–162

a) Use and form

Flying is exciting.
Fliegen ist aufregend.
Travelling makes me tired.
Reisen macht mich müde.

Als **Gerundium** *(gerund)* bezeichnet man die *-ing*-Form eines Verbs, wenn sie als **Nomen** verwendet wird.

Taking **a taxi** is quite expensive.
Mit dem Taxi zu fahren / Taxifahren ist ziemlich teuer.
Cycling **in New York** can be dangerous.
In New York Rad zu fahren / Radfahren in New York kann gefährlich sein.

Das Gerundium kann wie ein Verb erweitert werden, z.B. durch ein Objekt *(a taxi)* oder eine Orts- oder Zeitangabe *(in New York)*.
Im Deutschen wird das Gerundium oft durch einen Infinitiv mit „zu" oder durch ein Nomen wiedergegeben.

b) The gerund as subject and object

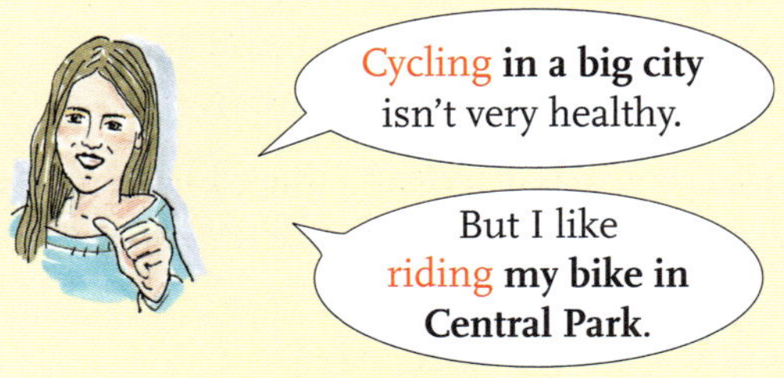

Das Gerundium (und seine Erweiterung) kann im Satz **Subjekt** oder **Objekt** sein:

Subjekt		
Flying	*is exciting.*	
Cycling in a big city	*isn't very healthy.*	
	Objekt	
My sister likes	***skating***.	
I like	***riding my bike in Central Park***.	

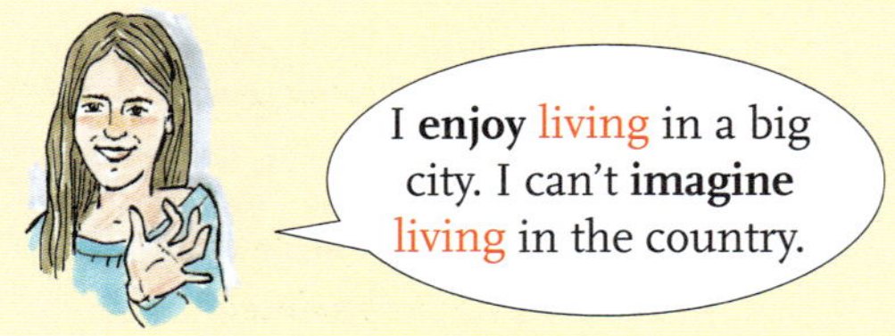

Ich wohne gern in einer Großstadt. / Ich genieße es, in einer Großstadt zu wohnen. Ich kann mir nicht vorstellen, auf dem Land zu leben.

When I got to Times Square, it **started** raining. / to rain.

I **like/love** riding / to ride my bike in the rain.

I'd like/love to ride in a New York taxi too.
I **would hate** to live in the country.

! Beachte:

◀ **1** Folgt bestimmten Verben – z.B. ***enjoy, finish, imagine, miss, practise*** – ein weiteres Verb, so steht es als Gerundium:
*I **enjoy** living ..., I can't **imagine** living ...*

Anders als im Deutschen darf nach diesen Verben **kein Infinitiv** stehen!
Also nicht: *I ~~enjoy to live~~ ..., I can't ~~imagine to live~~ ...*

◀ **2** Nach ***begin/start, continue, hate, like, love*** kann ein Gerundium oder ein *to*-Infinitiv stehen.

◀ **3** Nach ***would like, would love, would hate*** kann nur der *to*-Infinitiv stehen.

c) The gerund after prepositions

After so much walking, we were tired.
Nach all der Herumlauferei ... /
Nachdem wir so viel herumgelaufen waren, ...
Never cross a street without looking.
Überquere nie eine Straße, ohne zu schauen.

Ryan is **scared** of going in lifts.
Ryan hat Angst davor, mit dem Lift zu fahren.
Ryan was **excited** about going to the fire station.
Ryan freute sich darauf, die Feuerwache zu besuchen.

Nach einer Präposition *(after, without, for, of, ...)* steht ein Verb immer als Gerundium.

Beachte die verschiedenen deutschen Entsprechungen:

englisch	deutsch
– ***after walking***	→ „nach der Herumlauferei" *oder* „nachdem wir herumgelaufen waren"
– ***without looking***	→ „ohne zu schauen"
– *scared **of going ...***	→ „Angst, ... zu fahren"

Ryan is **interested** in learning about New York firefighters.
Ryan ist daran interessiert, etwas über ... zu erfahren.

They were **tired** of looking down at New York.
Sie hatten genug davon, auf New York hinabzuschauen..

Nützliche Wendungen mit Präposition + Gerundium sind:

– *(to) be* ***interested in / excited about / afraid of / good/bad at / tired of*** *doing sth.*

Ryan's **reason** for going to New York was to visit family. Sein Grund, dort hinzufahren, war ...

Caitlin had the **idea** of visiting the fire station.
Caitlin hatte die Idee, die Feuerwache zu besuchen.

Caitlin **was** against going to Brooklyn Bridge.
Caitlin war dagegen, zur Brooklyn Bridge zu gehen.

Ryan and Caitlin **talked** about meeting Ruth.
Ryan und Caitlin sprachen darüber, Ruth zu treffen.

–	the	***reason for*** ***idea of*** ***hope of*** ***danger of***	***doing*** *sth.*
–	*(to)*	***be against*** ***dream of*** ***talk about*** ***think of***	***doing*** *sth.*

Unit 2

GF 2 The passive

▸ *GF pp. 163–164*

a) Active and passive

Active: **Farmers in California** grow strawberries on huge farms.
Landwirte in Kalifornien bauen Erdbeeren auf großen Farmen an.

Passive: **Strawberries** are grown on huge farms.
Erdbeeren werden auf großen Farmen angebaut.

◂ Mit einem **Aktivsatz** drückst du aus, **wer oder was etwas tut**.

Subjekt	**Verb**	**Objekt**
Farmers in California	*grow*	*strawberries ...*

◂ Mit einem **Passivsatz** drückst du aus, **mit wem oder womit etwas geschieht**. Das Objekt des Aktivsatzes *(strawberries)* ist Subjekt des Passivsatzes geworden:

Subjekt	**Verb**	
Strawberries	*are grown*	*on huge farms.*

b) Form

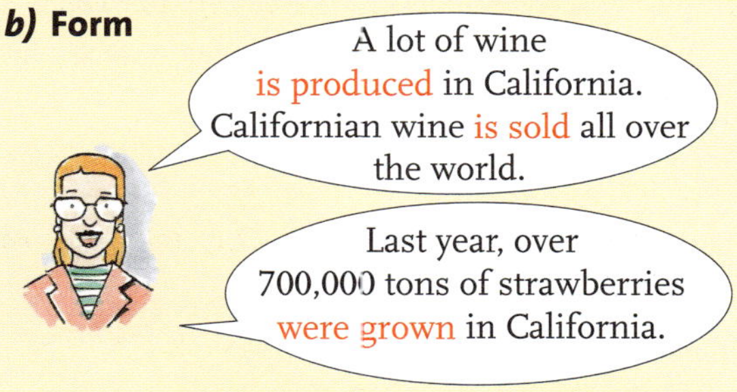

... wird produziert ... / ... wird verkauft ... / ... wurden angebaut ...

Das Passiv bildest du mit einer **Form von *be*** und der 3. Form des Verbs*.

Simple present: *am/are/is* + **3. Form des Verbs**
*A lot of wine is **produced** ...*

Simple past: *was/were* + **3. Form des Verbs**
*700,000 tons were **grown** ...*

* Die 3. Form des Verbs heißt **Partizip Perfekt** *(past participle)*. Sie wird bei regelmäßigen Verben mit ***-ed*** gebildet: *(to) produce, produced, produced*. Unregelmäßige Verben haben eigene Formen: *(to) grow, grew, grown*.

c) Use

At 8.45 yesterday morning a 12-year-old boy was hurt in a car accident on Duke Street. The police were called and the boy was taken to hospital.

In einem Passivsatz steht nicht, wer die Handlung ausführt. Oft ist das unwichtig oder gar nicht bekannt.
Du findest daher das Passiv oft in Nachrichten und in Zeitungsberichten (z.B. über Unfälle, Verbrechen) oder auf Schildern.

Ein englischer Passivsatz wird im Deutschen oft durch einen Aktivsatz mit „man" wiedergegeben:
*The boy **was taken** to hospital.*
***Man brachte** den Jungen ins Krankenhaus.*

d) Passive sentences with *by* ...

The gardener **was attacked** by a dog.
... wurde von einem Hund angefallen.

The Golden Gate Bridge **was built** by Joseph Strauss.
... wurde von Joseph Strauss erbaut.

My parents' house **was destroyed** by fire.
... wurde durch ein Feuer zerstört.

Wenn du in einem Passivsatz den „Täter" oder „Verursacher" nennen willst, verwendest du ***by*** („von", „durch").

e) Extra The passive: *will*-future and modal auxiliaries

Our new attractions will be opened soon.
... werden bald eröffnet (werden).

Coloma can be visited at any time of the year.
... kann das ganze Jahr über besucht werden.

The fire couldn't be put out.
... konnte nicht gelöscht werden.

Passivsätze mit Hilfsverben (z.B. *will, can, could, must, should, may*) bildest du mit *be* + Partizip Perfekt:

will	*be*	*opened*
can	*be*	*visited*
could	*be*	*put out*
must	*be*	...
should	*be*	...
may	*be*	...

Unit 3

GF 3 Countable and uncountable nouns

▸ GF p. 165

a) Countable nouns

a friend – two friends
a CD – lots of CDs
one hour – many hours

◂ Die meisten Nomen sind **zählbar**, d.h., sie kommen im Singular und im Plural vor.

b) Uncountable nouns

bread	Brot	**money**	Geld
butter	Butter	**music**	Musik
equipment	Ausrüstung	**news**	Nachricht(en)
health	Gesundheit	**sugar**	Zucker
homework	Hausaufgabe(n)	**traffic**	Verkehr
information	Information(en)	**water**	Wasser
milk	Milch	**work**	Arbeit

not: ~~a bread; breads~~
~~an information; many informations~~
~~a homework; two homeworks~~

◂ **Nicht zählbare** Nomen stehen **nie** im Plural.
Zu den nicht zählbaren Nomen gehören viele Bezeichnungen für Lebensmittel und viele abstrakte Begriffe, z.B. *health*.

! Auch die Nomen ***homework, information*** und ***news*** sind nicht zählbar – anders als ihre deutschen Entsprechungen.

That's too much **homework**. I can't do it.
Das sind zu viele **Hausaufgaben**. Ich kann sie nicht machen.

◂ Die zugehörigen **Begleiter, Verben und Pronomen** stehen immer **im Singular**.

Would you like a glass of **milk**.
Möchtest du **ein Glas Milch**?

◂ Wenn du **bestimmte Mengen** oder eine **bestimmte Anzahl** nennen willst, musst du passende Wendungen wie ***a glass of ..., a kilo of ..., a piece of ...*** verwenden.

c) Quantifiers: *some, a lot of, many, much*

Countable nouns	Uncountable nouns
some **students** einige/ein paar ...	some **bread/information** etwas Brot/einige Informationen
a lot of **students** viele ...	a lot of **bread/information** viel Brot/viele Informationen
how many **students?** wie viele ...?	**how** much **bread/information?** wie viel Brot? / wie viele Informationen?

Die Mengenangaben *some* und *lots of* (oder *a lot of*) verwendest du mit **zählbaren Nomen** und **nicht zählbaren Nomen**.

! – *many* heißt „**viele**" und steht nur mit **Nomen im Plural**.
– *much* heißt „**viel**" und steht nur mit **nicht zählbaren Nomen**..

GF 4 The definite article *the* ► *GF p. 166*

Wenn ein Nomen **ganz allgemein** gebraucht wird, steht es **ohne den bestimmten Artikel**.

Das gilt insbesondere für

1 For Timo and his family, life is exciting at the moment. ... ist das Leben im Moment aufregend.

1 **abstrakte Begriffe** wie *life, history, health, traffic*

2 Clean air is important to health.
Saubere Luft ist wichtig für **die** Gesundheit.

2 **Stoffbezeichnungen** wie *air, oil, gold, coffee, bread*

3 American students do lots of extracurricular activities.

3 **Nomen im Plural** (hier: *students*).

1a At the FFA meeting Timo learned a lot about the life **of Missouri farmers.**
... über das Leben der Farmer in Missouri.

2a The Schmidts are happy that the air **in Hermann** is clean. ... die Luft in Hermann

3a The students **who went to the FFA meeting** were very interested in hogs.

◄ Wenn diese Nomen aber **näher bestimmt** sind, stehen sie **mit bestimmtem Artikel**.
Die nähere Bestimmung erfolgt z.B. in Satz 1a durch eine *of*-Fügung *(of Missouri farmers)* und in Satz 3a durch einen Relativsatz *(who went to the FFA meeting)*.

Vergleiche die Sätze 1a–3a mit den Sätzen 1–3.

GF 5 The past perfect ► *GF p. 167*

a) Use

Andreas Schmidt first **visited** Hermann over 20 years ago. ... besuchte ...
He **stayed** with the Kruger family. ... wohnte ...

◄ Du benutzt das *simple past* für abgeschlossene **Handlungen, Ereignisse und Zustände in der Vergangenheit**.

Andreas Schmidt had never heard of Missouri wine when he **discovered** that Hermann had a lot of wineries.
... hatte noch nie von Wein aus Missouri gehört, ...

They had already sold their house in Germany when Karla Schmidt **got** worried.
Sie hatten ihr Haus in Deutschland bereits verkauft, ...

◄ Mit dem *past perfect* (Plusquamperfekt, Vorvergangenheit) drückst du aus, dass etwas noch **vor etwas anderem in der Vergangenheit** stattgefunden hatte.
Die Handlung/das Ereignis im *past perfect* geschah zuerst:

1.	**2.**
They had already sold ...	*when she **got worried**.*

b) Form

We had sold our house, so there was no way back.
They hadn't played soccer before.

Das *past perfect* bildest du mit ***had*** und der 3. Form des Verbs (Partizip Perfekt, *past participle*).

Had the Schmidts already moved to Hermann when Timo was 12?
Waren die Schmidts schon nach Hermann gezogen, ...?

! Beim *past perfect* musst du immer ***had*** verwenden, egal ob im Deutschen „hatte" oder „war" steht.

Unit 4

GF 6 *since* and *for* (German 'seit')

▸ *GF pp. 168–169*

a) The present perfect with *since* and *for*

Dad ist **seit** 1999 beim King Center.
Er kennt seinen Chef **seit** Jahren.

Du kannst das *present perfect* verwenden, um über einen **Zustand** zu sprechen, der in der Vergangenheit begonnen hat und jetzt noch andauert.

! Wenn du sagen willst, **seit wann** oder **wie lange** der Zustand bereits andauert, musst du aufpassen – es gibt zwei englische Wörter für das deutsche „seit“:

1. Mit *since* gibt du einen **Zeit**punkt an *(since 1999; since May; since 12 o'clock)*.
   ***since* + Zeitpunkt** drückt also aus, **seit wann** ein Zustand andauert.
   since+Zeitpunkt

2. Mit *for* gibst du einen **Zeit**raum an *(for years; for a month; for a long time)*.
   ***for* + Zeitraum** drückt also aus, **wie lange** ein Zustand bereits andauert.
   for+Zeitraum

***since* + Zeitpunkt** | ***for* + Zeitraum**

Madison and her mom are in the car on the way to the CNN studios. **It's 8.20.**

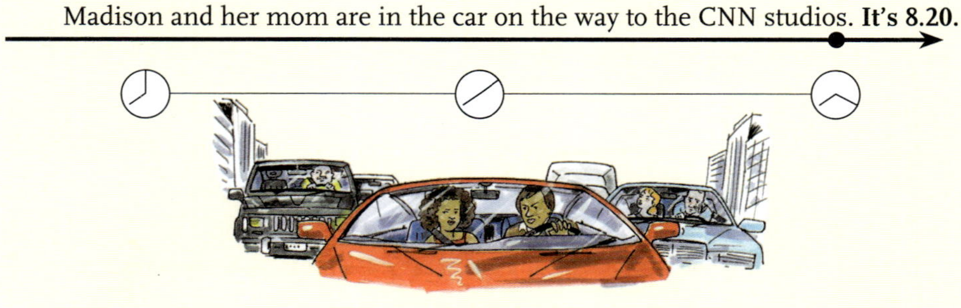

They'**ve been** in the traffic jam since 8 o'clock. ... seit 8 Uhr.

They'**ve been** in the traffic jam for 20 minutes. ... seit 20 Minuten.

We've lived in this house since 2004.
Wir wohnen seit 2004 in diesem Haus.

I've had my computer for three years.
Ich habe meinen Computer schon seit drei Jahren.

! Achtung:
Im **Deutschen** benutzt man meist das **Präsens**:
*Wir **wohnen** seit ... / Ich **habe** ... seit ...*

Im **Englischen** muss das ***present perfect*** stehen:
***We've lived** ... since ... / **I've had** ... for ...*

How long **have** you **lived** in Atlanta?
– Since 2005. / For a few years.

Wie lange **wohnt** ihr in Atlanta?
– Seit 2005. / Seit ein paar Jahren.

Mit ***How long ...?*** + *present perfect* fragst du, seit wann oder wie lange ein Zustand schon andauert.